SCULPTURE. Ron Franks. Red cotton and jute. *Courtesy, artist*

BUKKEH MUSHERSHUBEH. Neda Al-Hilali. Three-dimensional wall hanging from multiple yarns, cord, and other materials over a wire frame.
Courtesy, artist

BELT. Esther Parada. Jute and wool. *Photo, author*

VEST. Julia Littell. Rug yarn. *Photo, author*

MACRAMÉ

Creative Design in Knotting

Books by Dona Z. Meilach in Crown's Arts and Crafts Series:

COLLAGE AND ASSEMBLAGE
CONTEMPORARY ART WITH WOOD
CONTEMPORARY BATIK AND TIE-DYE
CONTEMPORARY STONE SCULPTURE
DIRECT METAL SCULPTURE
    with Donald Seiden
MACRAMÉ ACCESSORIES
MACRAMÉ: CREATIVE DESIGN IN KNOTTING
PAPIER-MÂCHÉ ARTISTRY
SCULPTURE CASTING
    with Dennis Kowal
SOFT SCULPTURE AND OTHER SOFT ART FORMS

Also:
ACCENT ON CRAFTS
THE ARTIST'S EYE
COLLAGE AND FOUND ART
    with Elvie Ten Hoor
CONTEMPORARY LEATHER: ART AND ACCESSORIES
CREATING ART FROM ANYTHING
CREATING ART FROM FIBERS AND FABRICS
CREATING WITH PLASTER
CREATIVE STITCHERY
    with Lee Erlin Snow
MAKING CONTEMPORARY RUGS AND WALL HANGINGS
PAPERCRAFT
CREATING DESIGN, FORM, COMPOSITION
    with Jay Hinz and Bill Hinz
PRINTMAKING
WEAVING OFF-LOOM
    with Lee Erlin Snow

DONA Z. MEILACH

MACRAMÉ

Creative Design in Knotting

CROWN PUBLISHERS, INC., NEW YORK

For:

Vivian, Seymour, and Floyd

LIBRARY OF CONGRESS CATALOG CARD NUMBER: 73-147330

PRINTED IN THE UNITED STATES OF AMERICA

Published simultaneously in Canada by
General Publishing Company Limited

Designed by Shari de Miskey

Seventeenth Printing, April, 1975

Acknowledgments

I am most indebted to all the artists whose work appears within the book. Knotters throughout the country shared their work and ideas with me and often referred me to others to help in the compilation of materials.

I also wish to thank Herb and Lee Snow, my Los Angeles hosts who provided contacts and a base for me to interview West Coast artists and photograph their output. Thanks, too, to Virginia Black for her photographic assistance, and to Joyce Wexler, whose all-around research, contacts, and modeling skills are deeply appreciated.

Special acknowledgment to my daughter, Susan Meilach, and my niece, Elyse Pearlman, who became my avid Macramé students so they could assist with knotting demonstrations while I photographed their hands at work.

Edward Sherbeyn, Sherbeyn Gallery, Chicago, and Linda Caldwell Kramer, American Crafts Council, New York, also provided invaluable leads to contemporary knotters.

Ben Lavitt, Astra Photo Service, Inc., Chicago, has my deep gratitude for his consultation and advice in achieving the consistent photographic print quality. To Marilyn Regula, my typist, goes my continuing admiration for her infinite patience in deciphering my mistyping.

How can I ever thank my husband, Dr. Melvin Meilach, for putting up with knotted cords and photographic equipment that displaced him from the family room for months?

Dona Z. Meilach
Palos Heights, Illinois

NOTE: *All photographs by the author unless otherwise credited.*

v

Contents

Acknowledgments   v
List of Color Plates   ix
Foreword   xi

1 MACRAMÉ . . . ARTISTRY WITH KNOTS   2
2 BEGINNING TO MACRAMÉ   14
Materials   14
Cords and Sources   15
The Starting Knot   20
    The Lark's Head   20
Basic Knots   22
    Clove Hitch: Horizontal, Diagonal, Vertical 22
    Square Knot   32
        Half Knot Twist   37
        Alternating Square Knot Patterns 40
        Square Knotting Variations 44
        Square Knot Buttons 51

3 WORKING METHODS   52
Tying Bundles and Butterflies   52
Measuring Cords   56
Keeping Records of Cords   57
Stiffening Cords   58
Color and Cords (Dyeing)   61
Adding Cords   64
Adding Beads and Other Things   70
What to Do with Ends   78
Wrapping   79

4 SOURCES AND IDEAS FOR
MACRAMÉ FORMS AND DESIGNS   84

5 SCULPTURAL MACRAMÉ   102
Methods for Beginning   103

6 VARIATIONS OF THE CLOVE HITCH   130
Clove Hitch Chains   130
Reverse Clove Hitch Chains   132
Lark's Head Chains   141
Solid Angled Clove Hitch   146
Berry Knot   150

7 INCREASING YOUR KNOT VOCABULARY   152
Overhand Knot   153
Josephine Knot   158
Monkey's Fist   160
Chinese Crown Knot   162
Coil Knot   163
Weaving   164
Tassels   166
Fringes   167

8 MACRAMÉ AND MIXED MATERIALS   170

9 FASHIONS AND ACCESSORIES   180

10 MACRAMÉ FURNISHINGS   196

Bibliography   202
Sources for Supplies   203
Index   207

List of Color Plates

WALL HANGING. Neda Al-Hilali.
frontispiece

SCULPTURE. Ron Frank.
frontispiece

BELT. Esther Parada.
frontispiece

VEST. Julia Littell.
frontispiece

PENDANT. Marci Zelmanoff.
facing page 116

SCREEN. Joan Michaels Paque.
facing page 116

SUN HANGING. Esther Dendel.
facing page 116

PONCHO. Edward Sherbeyn.
facing page 116

ALTERNATE SQUARE KNOT PATTERN. Dona Meilach.
facing page 117

BIB. Marci Zelmanoff.
facing page 117

VALANCES. Joan Michaels Paque.
facing page 117

WALL HANGING (detail). Joan Michaels Paque.
facing page 117

SWALLOWS NEST. Doris Hoover.
facing page 148

MACRAMÉ ON EXHIBITION. Claire Zeisler.
facing page 148

NECKLACES. Sally Davidson and Lynn Needham.
facing page 149

HIM. Louise Todd.
facing page 149

NECKLACES. Helen Hennessey.
facing page 149

FLOOR PIECE. Babs Burchall.
facing page 149

Foreword

Macramé: Creative Design in Knotting is a modern interpretation of an old technique. The knots used for Macramé are almost as easy as those we first tied in our shoelaces. It is the application that is new; and this book presents the infinite designs possible from tying knots using only your fingers: no needles, hooks, or tools.

The emphasis is on creativity, expressiveness, and investigation into the artistic possibilities of string, twine, yarn, rope, and other cords. It is a stimulating art form for serious artists and craftsmen and for teachers at almost every grade level. Macramé is an exciting approach to arts and crafts for camp programs and for hobbyists everywhere. Occupational therapists will find it invaluable. The resulting line-space relationships make Macramé an excellent technique for exploring pure form and design as well as for creating individualized utilitarian items: clothes, belts, purses, and furnishings. Once the knot procedures are learned, you can easily progress without any predetermined patterns. Knotting may also be a springboard to working with fibers and textiles in infinite ways.

Knotting demonstrations have been developed in a logical progression with easy-to-follow photographs. They are organized so you may refer to any knot or knotting direction quickly. All descriptive and instructional material accompanies the photos.

The basic Square Knot and Clove Hitch are quickly learned and mastered with a little practice; then one is ready to think in terms of design and object. The examples emphasize form, shape, and color in traditional and modern approaches. There is an entire chapter presenting sources for stimulating visual experiences adaptable to design and dimension in knotting.

It must be emphasized that names of knots differ from book to book, and those used were chosen so that reference to them would be easy and unobtrusive. Methods of tying some knots differ by authors, and so long as results were the same, the simplest method was elected.

Even if you never knot a finished piece, learning what Macramé is will help you appreciate the growing interest in textile arts. You'll be able to recognize the difference between a crocheted, woven, knitted, or knotted fabric; and this awareness can result in a greater appreciation of art techniques and creative uses of materials.

MACRAMÉ

Creative Design in Knotting

MACRA BIRD. Aurelia Muñoz. White cotton and linen, 36" high, 18" wide. Predominantly tied with Clove Hitches in varying directions.

2

Macramé...
Artistry with Knots

Macramé, an art form made by knotting cords in imaginative combinations, is capturing the attention of contemporary artists and craftsmen. Fibers normally associated with industrial and domestic use are being applied to an expressive art statement, thus adding a new chapter to the history of modern textile arts.

A work of Macramé may look complicated. Watching someone rapidly tie knots can be confusing. Actually, Macramé is one of the simplest techniques for creativity. It involves tying only two knots—the Clove Hitch and the Square Knot—knots you have probably used for years. They are among the first learned by every Boy and Girl Scout.

Macramé is easily mastered by young and old. No tools, complex studio, or working space are required. Materials—twine, rope or yarn, scissors, pins and a square of poly-foam or cork—are readily available. Your working area may be no larger than your lap. Knotting may be worked during odd waiting moments, while watching TV, sitting at a meeting, or traveling in a car, bus, or plane.

What is the origin of Macramé? It is an Arabic word meaning "fringe," and derives from an early practice of knotting a fringe to a solid fabric, then continuing to make a pattern of knots. Eventually, entire pieces of knotted fabric were made and these had a strong, lovely, lacelike texture used for doilies, altar cloths, and church vestments.

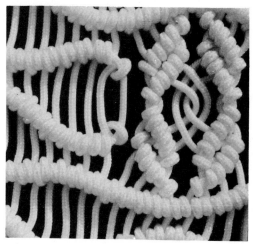

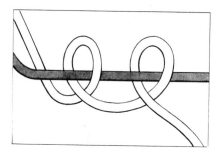

The Clove Hitch is a versatile knot that may be tied in many directions and combinations for an endless variety of designs and forms.

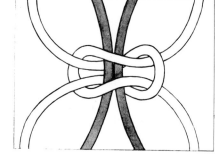

The Square Knot, so simple to tie, results in complex-looking, beautiful designs.

Photos, Henry Paque

The early history of Macramé is vague. There is some documentation that it was done in fifteenth-century France and Italy. It was most popular among nineteenth-century American and British sailors, who whiled away long shipboard hours tying thousands of Square Knots. They made fringes for bell and wheel covers used about the ship, for screens and nets, and for other decorative and functional purposes, often vying to develop new, unusual Square Knot combinations. But, as the radio became popular and books more plentiful, the knotting pastime faded.

ROWENA. Dorris Akers. Cotton seine twine #36, 43" long, 14" wide. In this traditional approach to Macramé, only the Clove Hitch and Square Knot are used with intermittent areas of floating, unknotted cords. Various patterns are achieved by changing the directions and sizes of the two basic knots.

Collection, Mr. and Mrs. Peter Emil Zehler

Departures from the symmetrical, flat concept of traditional Macramé have free, open appearance with great interplays of space.

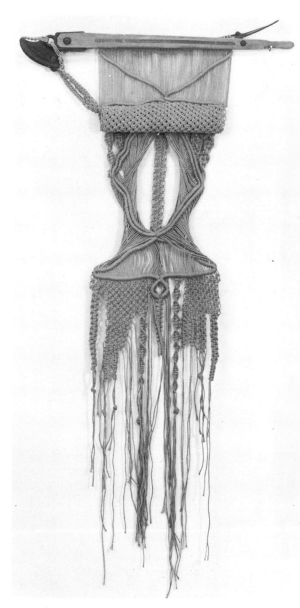

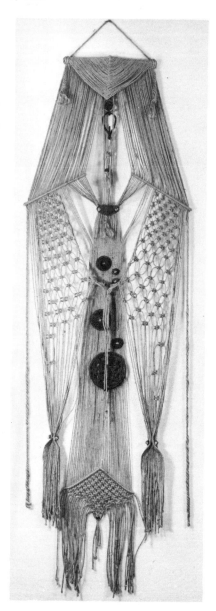

KNOTTING. Clara Creager. Natural jute knotted on a wood and iron handle, 76″ long, 36″ wide.

Collection, Jack Wilson, Columbus, Ohio,
Photo, Arthur Burt, Inc.

PISCES. Clara S. Dumas. Jute and found metal.

Courtesy, Philbrook Art Center, Tulsa, Oklahoma

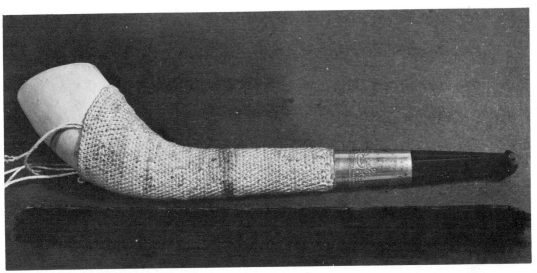

Cotton twine Square Knotted cover for a pipe. Typical of projects knotted by sailors.

Courtesy, The Mariners Museum, Newport News, Virginia

Through the early twentieth-century, belts, purses, leashes, lanyards, bell, light and shade pulls, and other strictly utilitarian objects were knotted in traditional designs and styles. In Portugal, Mexico, and Ecuador, local artisans still produce items such as purses and shawls as a native craft.

Among serious artists involved with modern "textile" arts, the potential of Macramé is being explored with unprecedented enthusiasm. Using the knotting technique, they are creating large wall-hangings and sculptures. They are combining knotting with other media and techniques such as weaving and stitchery, ceramics, and glass blowing.

Knotted practical items are popular, too. These reflect a free innovative approach to form and design. Purism and traditional patterns are often discarded as today's craftsmen strive to develop contemporary statements.

Artists are adapting scores of natural and man-made fibers that add texture and color for unusual combinations. Inevitably, there are differing theories. There are those who believe the knots themselves are the innate beauty and design of the finished piece; others maintain that the knots are only a means to an end that relies on shape, dimension, and texture for its statement. Examples of both theories are offered to stimulate varying approaches to the forms that can evolve from a technique as simple as tying knots.

KNOTTED DOILY. Djordje Sekulić. 14″ diameter. Unless one looks closely and recognizes the knots, this could be mistaken for lacework or crochet.

KNOTTED BASKET used on a ship. The base is knotted over wood rings or wire hoops to give it form.

Courtesy, The Mariners Museum,
Newport News, Virginia

CASCADE. Claire Zeisler. Natural jute, 30″ high. Free-standing sculptural Macramé composed completely of knotted and wrapped fibers; no other structural support. A contemporary statement using knotting to achieve shape.

Collection, Dr. Robert Sager, Peoria, Illinois,
Photo, Jonas Dovydenas

SHIP OF FOOLS.   Neda Al-Hilali. Beginning from a central rod, the wrapped and knotted bundles of combined hemp, sisal, and wool yarns are built into space.

Courtesy, artist

NECKLACE. Charlene Burningham. Tensolite cord with glass beads.

Photo, Robert Burningham

CHOKER. Esther Parada. White cotton butcher's twine with wood beads.

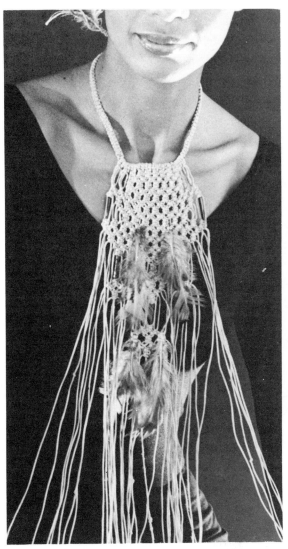

PRIMITIF. Joyce Wexler. Cotton wrapping twine with feathers.

Photo, Christa; for Ebony

Jewelry is among the exciting, innovative applications of modern Macramé. A necklace is a good beginning project for learning the knots. The work progresses quickly and the result may be worn. In these examples, only Clove Hitches and Square Knots are used, with beads or feathers added.

Other accessories developed imaginatively with Macramé are purses, belts, ponchos, and vests.

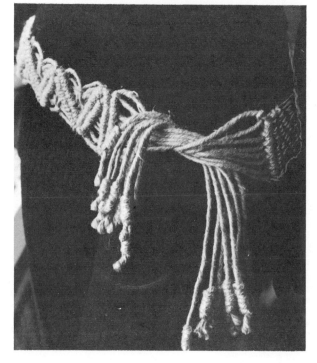

PURSE.   Mary Baughn. Blue rayon.

BELT.   Joan Michaels Paque. Jute.

PONCHO.   Esther Parada. Cotton twine with beads. Square Knots and Clove Hitches.

Photo, Christa; for Ebony

Beginning to Macramé

The basic materials required to begin knotting are minimal and accessible in local stores. You will need a knottting board, scissors, pins, and cord.

A knotting board may be anything that will hold a pin and be thick enough so when pins are inserted they do not go through the board and stick you. A twelve-inch square of polyurethane, sold in drapery departments and used for making accent pillows is excellent. Foam packing-material makes a good knotting surface; if the sheets are too thin, glue two together.

Other knotting boards might be several pieces of cardboard held together with glue or a rubber band, or two squares of cork glued for necessary thickness, or two self-stick carpet squares with a piece of board or cork between for rigidity. Celotex, a building material from a lumber-supply company, or any bulletin-board materials are especially good for large working surfaces.

T pins (also sold as wig pins) are available at sewing and notions counters. U-shaped pins, handy for holding heavy cords and bars to the board are sold at the do-it-yourself upholsterers' counters.

You can learn to make knots in any cord, string, or yarn. But you will be able to see how the knots form more readily if you use a fairly thick cord of nylon, cotton seine twine, or rug yarn. Use whatever you have handy to learn the knots and consider it a sampler.

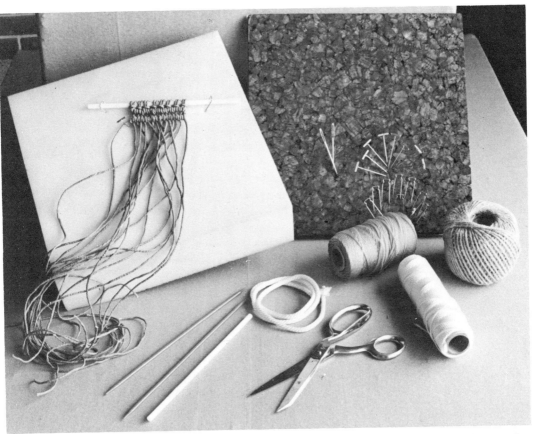

Materials for Macramé are a knotting board of polyurethane, cork, or other material that will hold pins; T or U pins, scissors, cord, and, optional but convenient, any kind of bar for mounting the cords. Shown are knitting needles, plastic straws, and cocktail stirrers. Darning or rug needles with large eyes are handy when wrapping ends and working in loose cords.

ABOUT KNOTTING MATERIALS

Macramé is essentially a "textile art," so technical knowledge of materials is helpful though not imperative. Many craftsmen work cords without really knowing what they are made of. Recently a few manufacturers have begun to label cords specifically for Macramé, but usually these are familiar materials such as polypropylene cord used industrially in other contexts.

Cords may be classified as *natural* and *man-made*. Natural cords are made from plants such as jute, sisal, manila, flax, hemp, cotton, raffia, and linen, wool from animals, and silk from worms.

Cords adaptable to Macramé are jute, sisal, hemp, cotton, seine twine, traverse cord, polypropylene, weaving warp, silk and rayon cord, decorative wrapping twine, cotton wrapping string, knitting worsteds, and rug yarn.

Man-made cords include assorted synthetic materials: rayon, nylon, plastic, Swistraw, polypropylene, polyethelene, wire wrapped in fibers, etc. The thicknesses, textures, and sometimes colors provide a marvelous choice.

The variety of cords is vast, and availability differs by locale. Therefore, seeking suppliers for various cords is often as important as specific supply sources. Twine, string, rope, yarn, etc., are found in abundance in hardware stores, cordage companies (listed in your telephone classified pages under that heading), marine stores, drapery sections of department stores, weaving suppliers, millinery outlets, craft and gift shops: wherever cord is sold for any use. Yarns, from thin multifilaments to rug yarns, are available from knit and craft supply centers

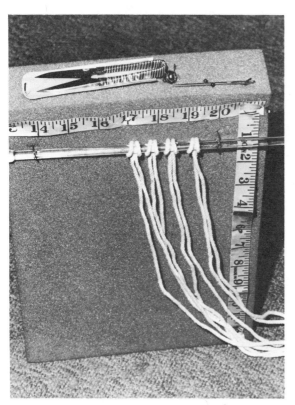

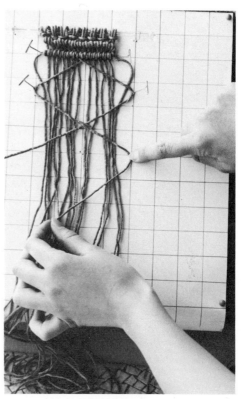

A foam kneeling pad, available in dime stores, is efficiently set up for knotting. A tape measure has been cut and pinned for measuring. A glass stirring rod held by U pins serves as a "holding line."

Two cork squares glued together and covered with paper marked off into 1" squares helps keep lines and angles of cords even. Pins are used to hold cords in place as they are worked.

and by mail from many suppliers (see page 203 for sources of supplies).

As you purchase cords, you'll observe that some are twisted from three or more lengths of fibers which are referred to as the "ply." A three-ply cord is composed of three separately twisted lengths; a five-ply cord will have five lengths of fibers twisted together. The number of plies to a cord has no bearing on its size; an eight-ply cotton twine used for wrapping may be quite thin, whereas a three-ply jute may be a thick cord.

Cords are also braided. The lengths of fibers, rather than being twisted, are worked into braids. These are particularly pretty in nylon and polypropylene having a high luster that resembles silk. Some are solidly braided; others may have a hollow core.

For large flat hangings, a Celotex knotting board is marked off in 1″ squares and placed on a table. Lengths of cord are wound into bundles for working convenience. T pins hold anchor cord and knots even.

Cords are measured by diameter and weight. Diameters may vary from ³⁄₃₂ of an inch to ¾ of an inch and thicker. Some balls of twine are sold by weight at so much per pound. They are sold also by the foot and yard. Yarns are usually marked by weight per skein as well as lengths.

In your early forays for cord, you will be most successful if you hunt for those labeled by use as well as type of material. You will find seine, mason and chalk line in abundance in many diameters in nylon and cotton, twisted and braided. All are excellent for Macramé. Look for wrapping and parcel-post twine, clothesline, sash cord, kite cord, upholsterer's cord, yacht braid, India twine. Buy a ball each of jute, sisal, and hemp and work them into knots to experience the differences in feel, practicality, color, and results.

Sometimes ropes are impregnated with oils and insecticides such as creosote and they have an odor. Should you discover an unusual color rope, smell it first to be sure the color is not simply a pungent additive rather than a dye.

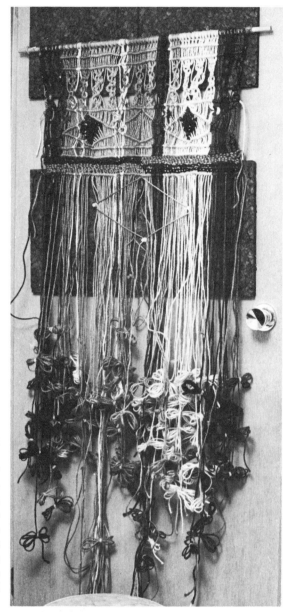

Self-stick cork squares are mounted on the inside of a door, and the work pinned to the boards. The knotting is raised as it progresses. Improvise any working space for a particular project; a hook in a doorway, a chandelier, a nail on a fence, over a door, anywhere convenient. For freely knotted and three-dimensional pieces, a knotting board is not necessary. You need only a place to hang the work and, perhaps, stones or washers at the bottom to weight and steady the anchor cords.

Color is a problem in Macramé. Available cords are often limited to natural shades of white, beige, and brown. Those that are not factory dyed you must dye yourself (see page 61). There are yellow cotton and nylon seine twine and earth-color traverse cords. Lily Mills now packages a polypropylene "macra-cord" dyed in six colors and a jute-tone available in approximately twenty colors. Weaving cords, embroidery rayons, and nylons do come in a range of colors, and working these in combinations can produce exciting results.

THE STARTING KNOT—THE LARK'S HEAD

The principle of Macramé is to interknot lengths of cords. For working convenience, knotting cords are mounted on a horizontal holding line such as a length of cord, dowel rod, knitting needle, or twig held to the board with pins.

To begin knotting, cut a minimum of eight cords, each approximately ten feet long. Fold them in half and mount on the holding line with a Lark's Head knot as illustrated. Eight folded cords result in sixteen working strands. It is difficult to estimate lengths of cords required for specific projects inasmuch as thicker cords are used up more quickly than thinner cords. Some directions for knotting deplete cord more quickly. A rough estimate is to cut cords four to six times the finished length desired, but this is not always valid. It depends on the number of knots used and how tightly they are tied. Experience is the best teacher. Don't panic should you run short of some cords; several ways to add cords are described in Chapter 3.

For photographic demonstrations, ¼″ nylon braid, cotton traverse cord, and cotton seine twine are used. They are strong enough to withstand tying and pulling, make an even knot, and mistakes are easy to discern and untie.

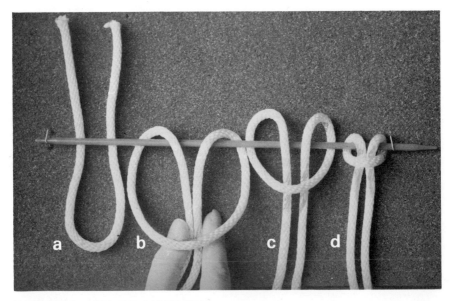

MOUNTING WITH THE LARK'S HEAD

a. Fold the cord in half and place loop under the horizontal holding line from top down.
b. Reach under the loop and over the horizontal line and grasp the two loose ends; bring them down through loop.
c. Pull and
d. Tighten.

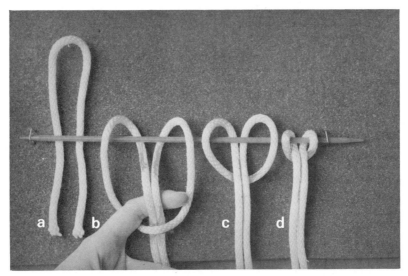

Reverse Lark's Head is used when the loop on the front of the pattern is not desirable.

a. Fold cord in half and place loop under horizontal line from bottom upward.

b. Fold loop over horizontal line; grasp free cords and bring them up through loop.

c. Pull and

d. Tighten for finished knot.

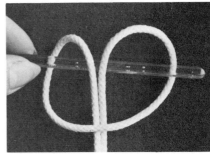

At right: With stiff cords, and as you become proficient, you can fold the cord over, then slip the holding line or rod through the loop.

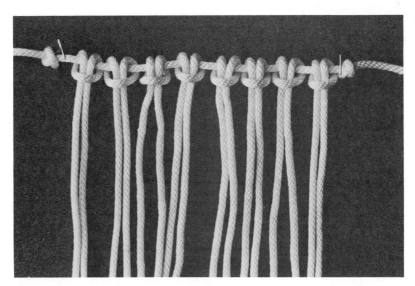

Eight cords ready for knotting mounted on a cord pinned tautly to a two-inch-thick polyurethane square pillow. To prevent the horizontal holding line from slipping, tie an overhand knot around the pin or pierce the cords with the pin. If this "sampler" is to be used as jewelry, make the holding line long enough to fit and tie around the neck.

BASIC KNOTS—THE CLOVE HITCH

Mastering the Clove Hitch (often called the Double Half Hitch) is absolutely essential to Macramé. This versatile knot is made with two loops; it may be tied in horizontal, vertical, and diagonal directions with many variations. The piece below is composed completely with Clove Hitches. By mastering the few demonstrations, you'll be able to read and duplicate any area of Macramé knotted with Hitches. The demonstration piece may be worn as jewelry or tacked on a wall. It is offered to help you become proficient in tying the Clove Hitch in varying directions.

When knotting, we will refer to "knotting cords" and "knotting strands" as those which are tied in knots. "Anchor cords" are those which knots are tied around.

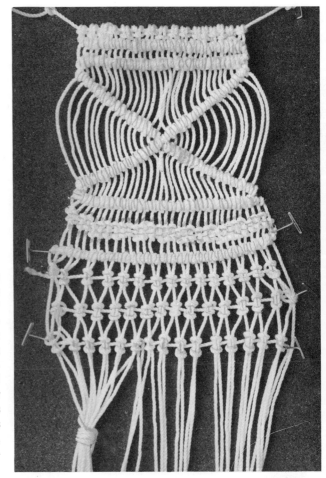

For this sampler, sixteen ⅛-inch nylon braid cords are mounted to provide thirty-two knotting strands. However, for photographic clarity, the actual demonstration has only eight cords (sixteen strands) of ¼-inch nylon braid. Work with as many cords as you like, depending upon the width of the finished piece desired. Use multiples of four cords: 8-12-16-20, etc. Begin with cords about ten feet long before doubling as they are easy to handle. Add rows, change directions, or alter the progression as you like.

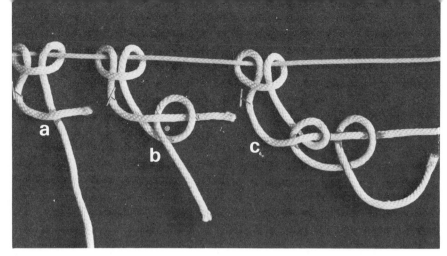

HORIZONTAL CLOVE HITCH tied *left* to *right* involves tying two loops around an anchor cord.

a. Pin the left strand of the first cord as shown and place it on *top* of all the cords. This becomes the "anchor cord" around which each strand will be knotted in turn for a horizontal bar.
   Always begin the knotting strand *under* the anchor cord and *hold or pin the anchor cord taut*.

b. Bring the knotting strand from under the anchor, loop it over and around to the left and through the loop as shown. This is the first half of the Clove Hitch. Tighten the loop.

c. The second half of the knot is made to the right of the first loop. It begins *over* the anchor cord, loops around to the left, and through as shown.

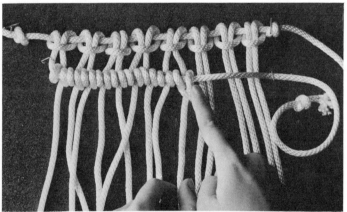

Continue to tie *each* strand *individually* around the anchor cord using the two loops of the Clove Hitch. As each loop is tied, push it next to the previous loop to achieve an even appearance. Tie a small knot in the end of the anchor cord to identify it and avoid confusing it with the knotting strands.

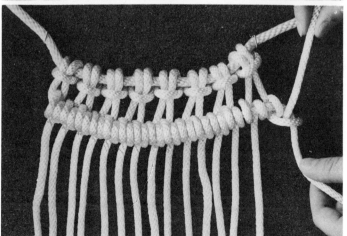

If the anchor cord is not held taut the Clove Hitch will tend to knot *with* the anchor cord, rather than over it. The loop will form at the bottom as shown on end knot; it will lack the even appearance of correctly knotted loops over a tautly held anchor.

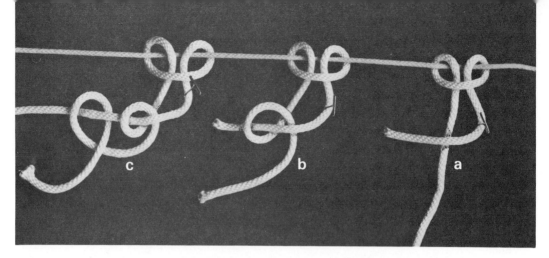

HORIZONTAL CLOVE HITCH *right* to *left*. To create a second bar, the Clove Hitch is worked in reverse from right to left, using the same anchor cord pinned or held taut across all the strands.

a. Hold or pin the anchor cord taut over the knotting strands. Begin knotting with first strand on the right next to the anchor cord.

b. Loop the knotting strand from *under the anchor* around, over, and through as shown. Tighten.

c. Bring knotting strand over the anchor cord and to the left of the first half of the knot for the second loop, working it around and through as shown. Continue to tie each strand individually around the anchor to complete a bar knotted from right to left.

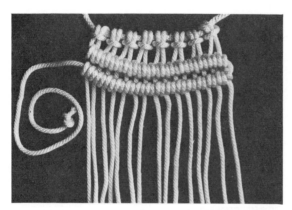

The finished two horizontal bars will appear like this. You will discover that the cord used for the anchor shortens more rapidly than the knotting cords. With experience, you will learn to plan for anchor cords and make them longer than knotting cords.

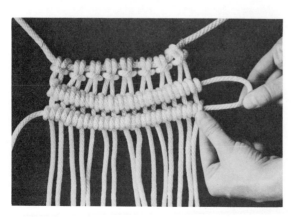

When knots are correctly tied, the anchor can be pulled through the knots readily. If the anchor does not pull through, and knots are uneven, it's because the anchor was not held taut as knotting progressed. This is also the way to rip out a horizontal bar rather than untie each Clove Hitch individually.

DIAGONAL CLOVE HITCH

To make diagonal rows, the same Clove
Hitches are used; *only* the angle at which
the anchor cord is held changes. The
direction of the anchor cord is the whole
secret to creating the myriad designs
you'll observe illustrated.

Pin the cords to the board in the diagonals desired; here they are crossed
over. Then use the same Clove Hitches
from right to left or left to right, knotting
on the diagonally held anchor cords.

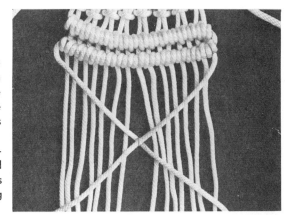

Beginning with the outer strands, Clove
Hitches are tied from left to right on
the left diagonal anchor cord; and from
right to left on the opposite side. Any
cord may become a new anchor cord
at any place in the knotting. For a true
diamond pattern, pick out the two center cords for anchors and pin each to
one outer edge. Clove Hitch over them
beginning with the inner strands and
then pin the anchors back to the center
again.

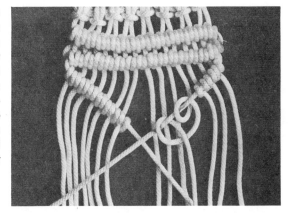

Finished crossover pattern with anchor
cord pinned to accept next horizontal
bar. Bars act as organizing elements
for design. It makes no difference which
anchor cord from the crossover is used.
If one becomes too short, pick up a
cord from the other side.

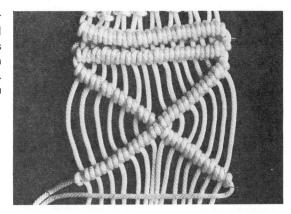

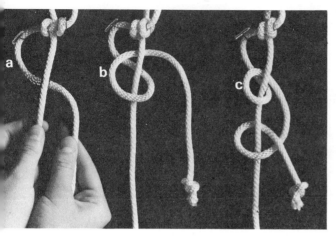

VERTICAL CLOVE HITCH, *left* to *right*

The Clove Hitch also may be tied vertically. For Vertical Hitches, the cord formerly used for the anchor changes its role and becomes the knotting cord. Because this one cord is used continuously for knotting it is used up very rapidly. When planning pieces with Vertical Clove Hitches, make the anchor cord much longer than any other cord. Each vertical cord, in turn, serves as an anchor cord for the vertical Clove Hitch. Vertical Hitching usually follows horizontal bars.

a. Place a pin at left edge of work to hold the knotting cord. Bring the knotting cord (formerly the anchor cord) *under* the first vertical strand on the left.

b. Loop the knotting cord over the new vertical anchor to the front, then around and through for the first half of the knot.

c. The second half of the knot is looped over the vertical cord and around as shown.

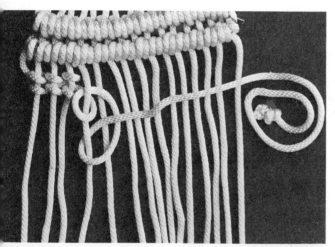

Continue the Vertical Clove Hitch by placing the knotting cord *under* each vertical strand and Clove Hitching with the same cord each knot.

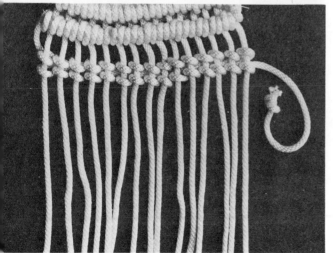

The completed row of Vertical Clove Hitches from left to right.

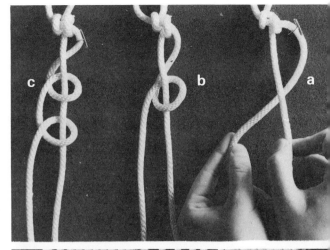

VERTICAL CLOVE HITCH, *right to left*

This involves exactly the opposite procedure of that described at left.

a. Pin the knotting cord at the right edge of the work and bring the knotting cord *under* the vertical strand at the right.

b. Loop the knotting cord to the right over the vertical strand, around and through at the top of the loop.

c. Make the second half of the Hitch over the anchor to the right, around the top of the loop and through. Continue by bringing the knotting cord under each strand and repeating the directions of the loops for the knot until the row is completed.

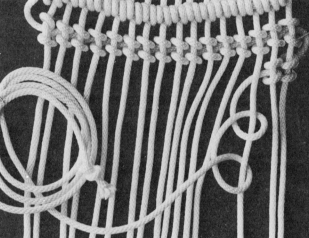

When one cord is used for knotting it shortens very rapidly. If necessary, introduce a new cord to begin the next row by pinning it to the board. Later you can tie, stitch or glue these ends together at the back of the work.

Because Vertical Clove Hitches use up cord quickly, the bar following such a series is also a good place to add new cord unobtrusively. It may be added only for the anchor for a bar, or it may be a long cord introduced as a continuing anchor or knotting cord. With experience and ingenuity for adding and hiding cords, you'll soon learn how to handle the problem. Additional suggestions on pages 64 to 69. Here, knotting is done with cotton seine twine.

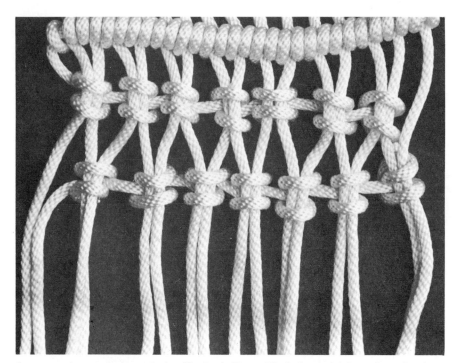

An attractive variation of the Vertical Clove Hitch is done by tying the knot over two vertical anchor cords at a time. For the first row, beginning at the left, tie a Vertical Clove Hitch over each pair of strands with one strand remaining at the end. Begin the second row from the right using this leftover cord in the first pair of strands and work right to left. Continue for as many rows as desired. The result is intricate looking but simple using alternate pairs of anchors. Vary the appearance by tying the rows close together or far apart.

Once you learn to do the Clove Hitch in its basic directions, you can achieve infinite variety by altering the direction of the anchor cord, by picking up new anchor cords, and by working groups of even and uneven rows. With this experience, you should be able to analyze any Clove Hitch pattern and work it out with only a little experimentation. Always strive to develop your own patterns.

Often the same patterns of knotting appear very different in different cords. Colors, too, affect the appearance of the knots. For more variations of the Clove Hitch, refer to Chapter 6.

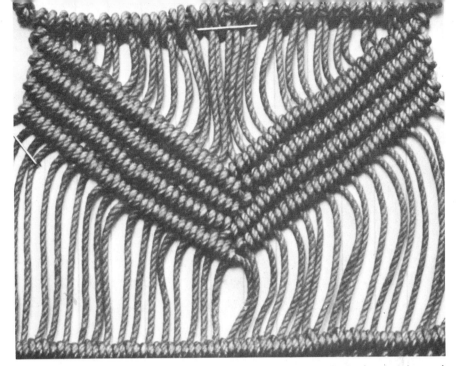

The Clove Hitch in chevron patterns worked in navy cord. To begin, the end cords are crossed over to the center to become the diagonal anchors for the vertical cord. For the second row, the next cords on each side become the anchors, then the next end cords become anchors for as many rows as desired. The anchor cords that remain in the center change their role and become knotting cords. Smooth out and place cords in order before tying next horizontal bar.

A crossover with an extra arm of the cross within. Knotted in braided nylon.
Photo, Henry Paque

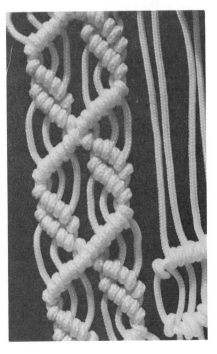

Another pattern of diagonal Clove Hitches. Anchor cords are selected as the pattern deems necessary. Cotton seine twine.

MACRA BIRD (detail of hanging on page 2) Aurelia Muñoz. Cords are worked around and toward the center where the ends emerge as a cascade. All knotting is the Clove Hitch in two cords, cotton and linen, and executed in the horizontal and vertical knotting techniques.

Courtesy, Galeria Juana Mordo, Madrid, Spain

#27. Rosita Montgomery. Natural jute twine and black horsehair. All diagonals of the Clove Hitch used for the sampler are employed here. Colors are carefully worked in so they emerge and disappear. Added ends are left frankly exposed for textural interest. A cowbell and stones are added.

Photo, Lee Payne

SQUARE KNOT AND HALF KNOT

The Square Knot is the second basic Macramé knot. There are different ways to tie the Square Knot, so if you have learned to do it by other steps than those shown, it's perfectly legitimate. Patterns and combinations for Square Knotting are infinite and limited only by the imagination.

The basic Square Knot is tied with four cords. The two inside strands are anchor cords and the outside strands are knotting cords. The Square Knot procedure illustrated involves the same steps; first to the left of the anchor cords, then to the right. A completed Square Knot will always lie flat—as shown in the two flat hangings at right which are tied mainly with the Square Knot and only a few Clove Hitch bars. When only one half of the Square Knot (a Half Knot) is tied in several successive ties, the result will automatically twist as illustrated in the large twisted rope at right.

Variety in Square Knotting is achieved in many ways. Basically the knots may be tied loose or tight, long or short, close together or far apart and intertwined with adjacent knots. Sennits (lengths of tied knots) may be overlapped and beads may also be incorporated.

It isn't necessary to adhere to a four-strand pattern, as you'll observe from the illustrations. Tie with six strands, eight strands, etc. Tie several strands over a multiple of anchor cords or multiple strands over two anchor cords. Tie large Square Knots over smaller ones. Be as inventive as you like.

Because Square Knots break down into four-cord multiples, mounting cords in amounts divisible by four simplifies designing. With freer designs, as opposed to controlled patterns, this is not so important. Also, if a cord is missed, dropped, depleted, etc., one can knot two cords together, add a cord, or somehow improvise so all is not lost.

The best way to learn the potentials of the knot is to practice tying it on sample cords. You may wish to continue working the remaining lengths from the Clove Hitch sampler or mount a minimum of six cords (twelve knotting strands), each about ten feet long, on a horizontal holding line and learn the Square Knot by following the directions. (To make the illustrations easier to follow, two color cords are used.) Soon, you'll be able to look at a pattern of Macramé and see, at a glance, how the knots were formed.

ASSORTED MACRAMÉ. Babs Burchall. Square Knots and Half Knot twists create the entire design in both flat hangings. The twisted sennit results when only one half of the Square Knot (Half Knot) is tied continuously.

THE SQUARE KNOT PROCEDURE

The Square Knot becomes second nature after you tie only a few. Showing knotting steps in photos or diagrams may appear involved, but be assured that after tying half a dozen or so knots, you'll have it mastered. Begin with four cords. Tie with the two outside cords over two center anchor cords.

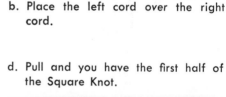

a. Bring the right cord *over* and to the left of the two anchor cords.

b. Place the left cord *over* the right cord.

c. Bring the left cord *under* the anchors and *through* the loop formed by the right cord.

d. Pull and you have the first half of the Square Knot.

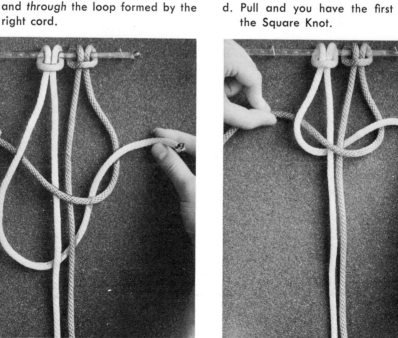

For the second half of the knot, follow the same procedure but on the right side of the anchor cords. To remember the knot, it helps to break the procedure down to a simple mnemonic device such as: to the left: over, over, under, and through. To the right; over, over, under, and through.

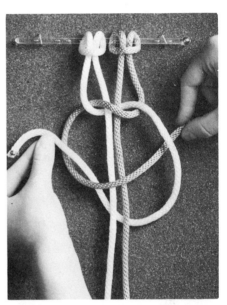

e. Bring the left cord *over* and to the right of the two anchor cords and place the right cord over it.

f. Bring the right cord *under* the anchors and *through* the loop formed by the left cord.

g. Pull the cords and . . .

h. The finished knot.

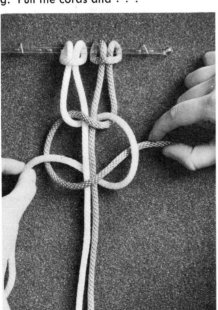

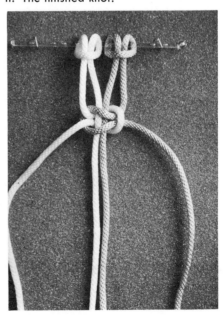

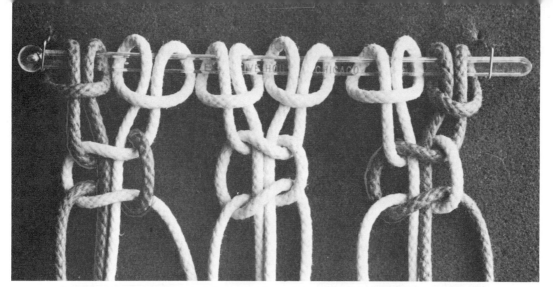

A row of Square Knots showing how the colors move from one side to another. The beginner may find knot formation easier to follow when two color cords are used such as this white and brown traverse cord. Anytime you must interrupt your knotting, it's easy to determine on which side to pick up the knot. If the last high ridge is on the right (as above) the next tie will begin to the left of the anchor cords. If the last high ridge is on the left, begin your next tie to the right of the anchor cords.

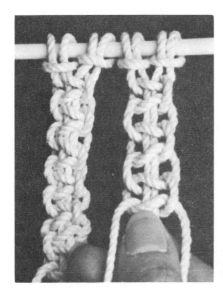

Properly tied Square Knots will slide easily up and down the anchor. To untie Square Knots, pull out the anchor cords at the top of the sennit, then undo the knotting cords.

After tying sennits of Square Knots, straighten and flatten out the cords so they may be tied in the proper order onto an organizing horizontal bar of Clove Hitches.

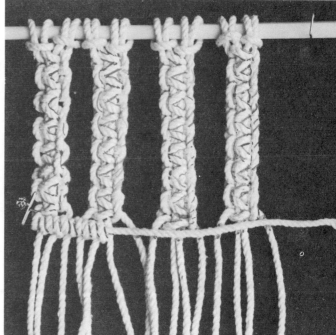

HALF KNOT TWISTS

Twisted sennits make an attractive motif. They occur automatically when you tie a series of Half Knots: that is, tie one half of the Square Knot continually. A full twist requires about seven Half Knots. When it begins to twist after the fourth knot, simply turn the sennit over and let the original first and fourth knotting cords reverse their positions.

Twists may be used in simple rows, crossed over, incorporated into the center of a large Square Knot. They may be tied with more than four strands. Practice a few twists, then observe how they are used in examples throughout the book.

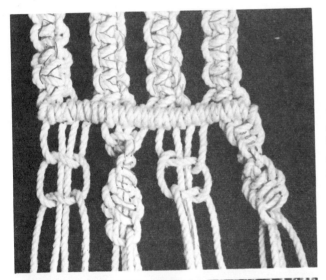

When Half Knots are tied to the left of the anchor cord, the knots twist left. When they are tied to the right of the anchor cords, they twist right. Cotton seine twine.

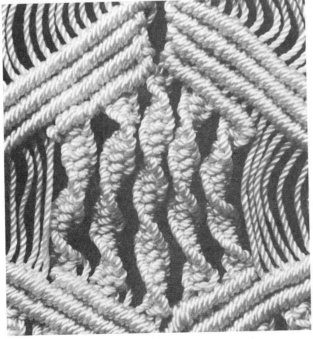

Long sennits of Half Knots result in multiple twists. Be sure cords from sennits lie in correct order before Clove Hitching a horizontal bar. Nylon seine twine.

More ways to work with Square Knots:

After tying a few Square Knot patterns, you'll soon be able to analyze what is happening in a design.

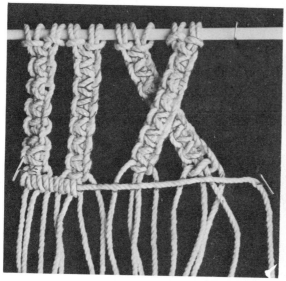

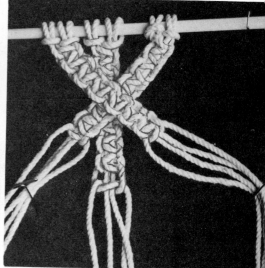

Two sennits may be crossed over for variety in Square Knotting design. Crossovers alternated with straight and twisted sennits are interesting. Cotton seine twine.

Three sennits may be crossed also. The two outer sennits will require more knots to even them up for use with a following horizontal bar.

Square Knot sennits are used straight and crossed followed by a double row of diagonal Clove Hitch bars. Observe the difference in the materials used. Nylon seine twine.

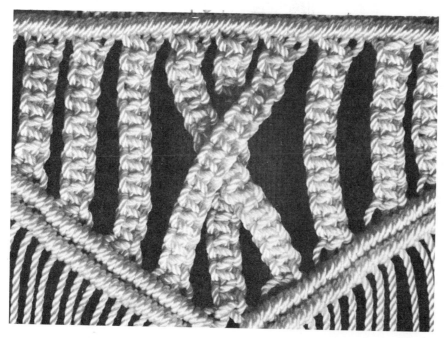

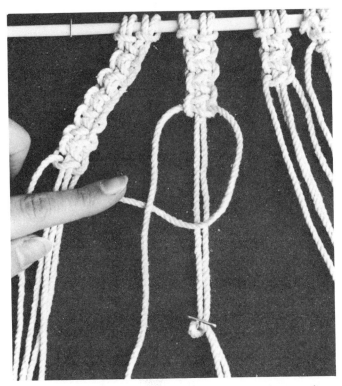

When tying rows of Square or Half Knots, it is sometimes faster to keep the anchor cords taut by pinning them to your board below your knotting area. Eileen Bernard holds them between her knees. Claire Zeisler ties them around her waist. Some knotters report tying them to their toes.

Sennits of Square Knots may be used as weaving within a pattern. Jute-tone cord.

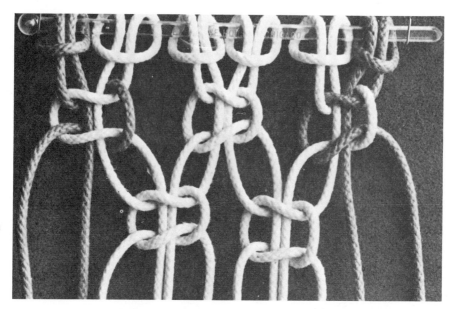

THE ALTERNATING SQUARE KNOT pattern is so simple to do and to vary that it is a basic pattern to all Macramé. Once learned, you will be able to recognize it in many variations and types of cords.

For the first row, make Square Knots in the usual way with four cords each. For the second row, drop the first two cords: then Square Knot with the next four cords. Knot each next group of four cords until the row is completed with two cords remaining at the end.

For the third row, pick up the first four cords again at the left and knot as in the first row. Continue the pattern by dropping the first two cords in each even-numbered row.

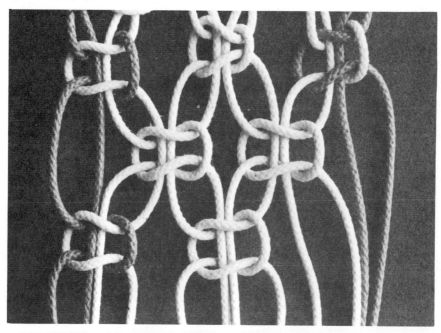

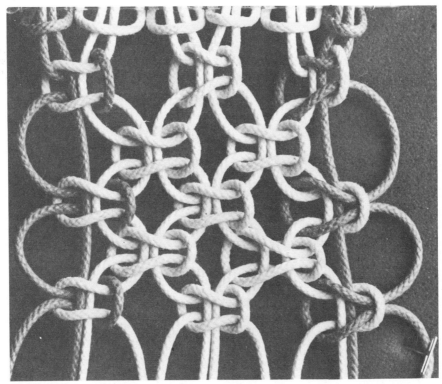

The design of alternate Square Knots is easy to follow in two colors of stiff traverse cord. For additional pattern interest, end cords may be pinned out in an accentuated curve. Other variations might be two knots in the even rows, combined with single knots in the odd rows. Study the examples for more possible patterns.

Alternate Square Knots with areas of floating cords create another pattern. #72 cotton seine twine.

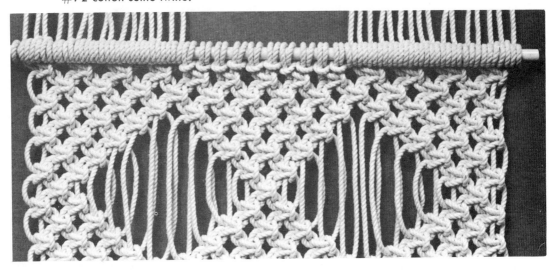

MACRAMÉ WITH ANTIQUE MIRROR. Berni Gorski. Cotton traverse cord. 27 inches long, 16 inches wide. Mainly Clove Hitches with patterns of alternating Square Knots. Bottom section utilizes basic knot variations (illustrated in Chapter 6) and Wrapping (Chapter 3). Observe how the sections at right and left of mirror are added by mounting new cords on the verticals and working an entire section in diagonal Clove Hitches to expand the total design.

Photo, Henry Gorski

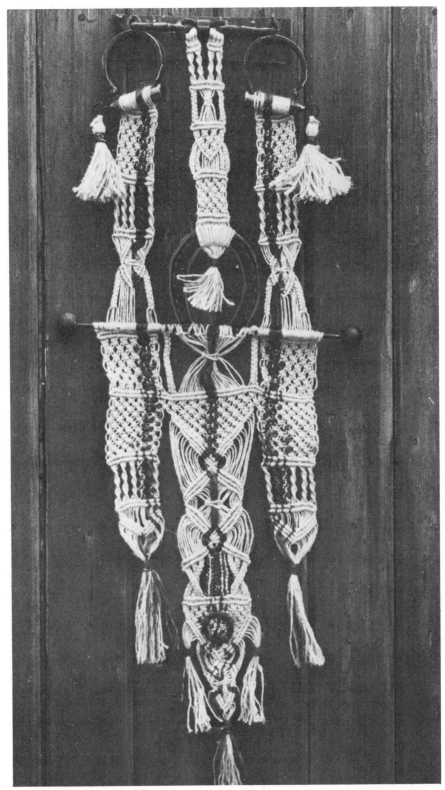

GOOD LUCK MACRAMÉ. Eileen Bernard. 42" long, 14" wide. White with black jute worked from stirrups welded to a found piece of metal. A horseshoe and metal rings also illustrate the trend to found object art and away from the pure cord compositions. New cords are added in the middle of the central bar to reestablish the pattern below the horseshoe.

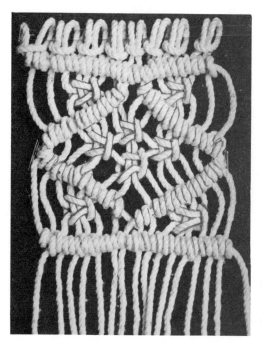

Square Knots tied before tying a pattern of the top diagonals of a diamond pattern. Alternate Square Knots tied within the diamond and also at the bottom carry out the design.

Using twelve cords for one pattern, tie two Square Knots with the eight central cords using four for an anchor. Then using those eight cords for anchor cords, knot a large Square Knot with the two cords on each side so a pattern of small and large Square Knots results.

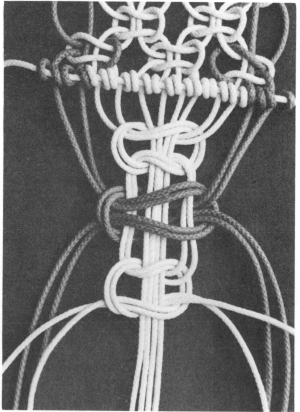

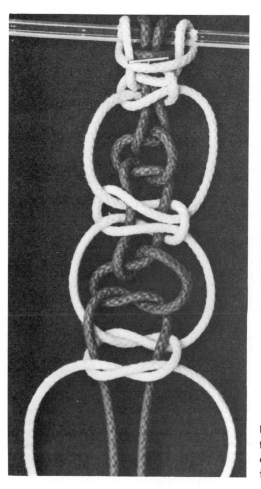

Using four cords, tie one Square Knot, then knot the two inner anchor pairs and tie another Square Knot with all four cords again.

Beginning to Macramé

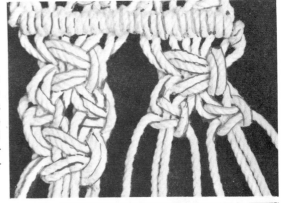

With eight cords, tie two outer pairs over four anchor cords. Then separate the anchors into two sets of four cords and tie two Square Knots on each side with each set. Bring together again and repeat the first knot using two outer pairs of cords over the four anchor cords.

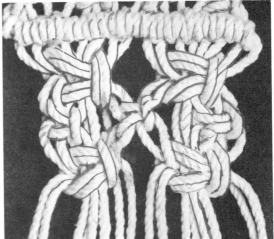

Another effect is possible by tying as in the procedure above, but this time connect the right two cords from the left sennit with the left two cords of the right sennit. Pattern of interconnected knots is complex looking, but simple and fun to do.

Sennits of Square Knots intertwined are easier to study and figure out than to describe verbally. Observe that the second and fourth sennits could easily be added cords at this point without affecting the continuity of the design.

By knotting sennits of varying multiples **A** of cords, it is possible to allow space for other sennits to be worked through. Try this with eight cords, but separate and tie them into two sets of four where you wish a hole to occur.

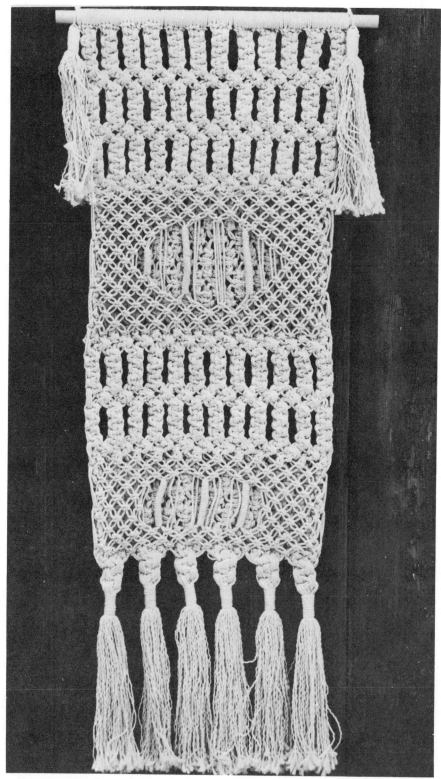

WHITE MACRAMÉ. Joy Lobell. Cotton seine twine, 38″ long, 14″ wide. Square Knots tied with multiples of four, six, and twelve strands. Two sections are double layered. For fringing, the plies of the twine have been unwound.

Detail of White Macramé on opposite page:

Top Square Knots tied with six cords (twelve strands). Sennits of four knots are worked into one row of alternate knots, then long sennits and alternating pattern repeated. For the second section the cords are separated into two layers front and rear.

Detail showing two layers:

Rear layer is of alternating Square Knots tightly tied with eight strands. Front layer is alternating Square Knot pattern tied loosely with four strands.
Floating cords and Wrapping (page 78) are used in the interior negative area so the rear pattern is visible.

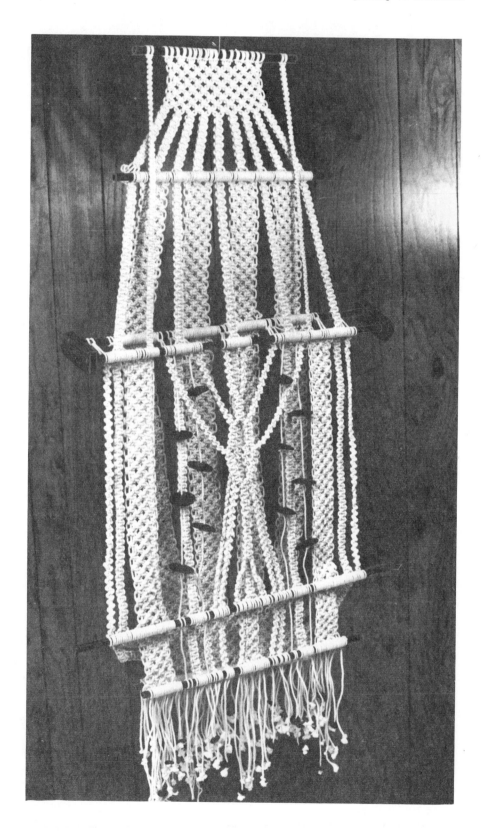

MACRAMÉ KNOTTED ON IRON AND WOOD HAME. Clara Creager. 38" long,
33" wide. Natural jute and rawhide laces in Half Knot twists and Square Knots.
Rawhide cords, cords are Square Knotted around anchor cords of jute.

Collection, Mr. and Mrs. Thomas McCollough,
Columbus, Ohio
Photo, Arthur Burt, Inc.

HANGING. Esther Robinson. Cotton seine twine, 58" long, 57" wide. Alternating
Square Knot patterns and Square Knot sennits. Wood dowels, used for the
horizontal bars, are attached with Clove Hitches. Wood discs have holes
drilled. Wood dowels and discs are dyed with India ink. The artist evolves
the design as she works in contrast to drawing it first and then developing
it from the drawing.

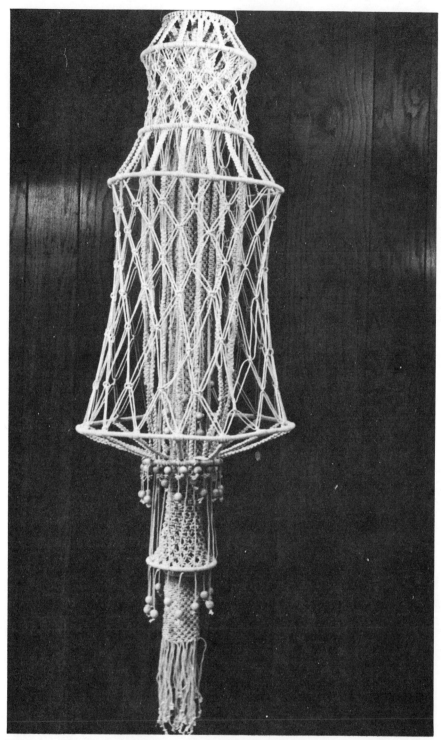

YELLOW HANGING. Esther Robinson. Yellow cotton seine twine with wood
beads, 46" long, 18" diameter. Three-dimensional Macramé is worked exactly
as flat pieces but mounting is on a welded metal ring rather than a straight
line. Multiple layers are achieved by working from two sets of rings knotted
one inside another. The two layers are worked simultaneously. The piece was
developed and larger rings added as the knotting progressed. See Chapter 5
for additional sculptural Macramé. Work might be hung from hooks in a ceiling, between a doorway, wherever there is freedom for the piece to hang.
Once knots are learned, a pinning surface is not so essential.

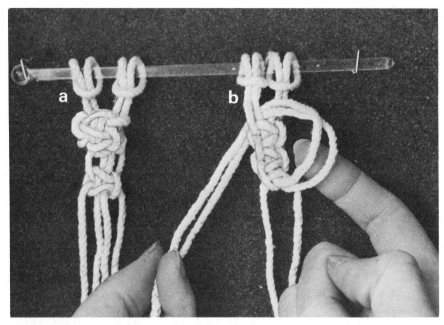

For additional surface texture on flat and dimensional Macramé work, use the Square Knot Button (a). (b) Tie a minimum of three Square Knots. (More for thicker buttons.) Bring the two anchor cords up over the knots and between the anchor cords at the top. Pull through to form the raised area. Continue knotting as at the bottom of (a).

Square Knot Buttons add surface and texture interest. They may be made large or small or in a progression of sizes.

3

Working Methods

There is no one best way to work with the many cords involved in knotting. Methods preferred by one person may not work so well for another. A particular project may require a new procedure. The following ideas for solving mechanical problems of Macramé are the result of interviews, observations of knotters at work, and experiences of those who teach Macramé.

Handling multiples of long cords so they do not tangle can be easily overcome. Wrap individual cords into bundles (called "butterflies") that will slide along the cord, releasing the length as it is needed. These may be self-tied or tied with rubber bands. Butterflies are sometimes awkward to work through loops, but they do eliminate pulling very long cords constantly. A sliding Clove Hitch is also demonstrated. For beginning students, some teachers recommend cords of convenient pulling length without bundling.

Measuring necessary lengths of cords can be efficiently accomplished in several ways. One knotter measures a required distance between two doorknobs, winds the cord over the two knobs, then cuts the cords at only one end. Cords on the other knob already are "halved" and ready for mounting.

A weaver's warping board is handy for measuring, if available, but other setups may easily be improvised. Place a wooden spoon handle upright in a kitchen drawer. Put the spool of twine on the handle and pull the cord into necessary lengths, using a premeasured distance

Large piece in progress is easier to work when cords are tied in bundles. They also may be wound around small bobbins used for knitting.

Courtesy, Estelle Carlson

along the counter. Set two C-clamps on a table or workbench with a tape measure stretched between.

Keeping records of cords is wise. Staple a sample of each cord to an index card and note where it was purchased, the price, and the colors in which it is available. Knot a small sample of the cord and determine how many cords produce an inch of knotting. This is like making a sample gauge in knitting.

Working with color gives an exciting dimension to Macramé. When buying colored cord or yarn, always overestimate your needs so you can buy one dye-lot. When dying your own fibers, always dye enough. It's frustrating to run short of cord and be unable to buy more of the same color or to achieve the same hues in your own dyes.

Several suggestions for adding cords—one of the bugaboos of beginning knotters—are offered. Fabric glues are indispensable when working large pieces. No matter how carefully one calculates, there always is the possibility of some cords shortening too fast. Frequently,

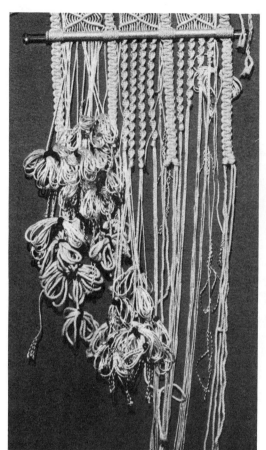

Sally Davidson ties bundles in "butter-fly" manner *(shown below)* and wraps each with a rubber band. When the bundle is pulled gently, additional cord is accessible for tying *(above)*.

To tie a butterfly: wind cord around two fingers, beginning the wind at a convenient length below the knotting. Do *not* wind from the bottom end first or cord will not pull out as needed. If you work with double or triple cords, wind these multiples into one bundle.

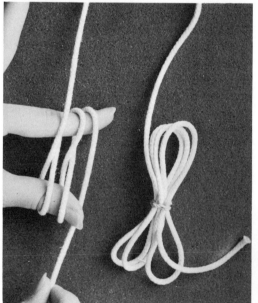

Some people find the large bundles cumbersome for pulling through knots. Cords also may be shortened for working convenience by Clove Hitching the end of a cord onto a point midway up. Then simply slide the hitch along the cord as you require extra length.

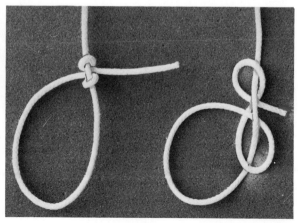

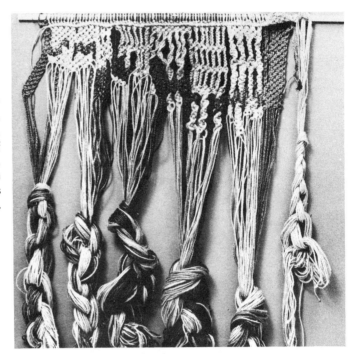

Julia Littell works this large piece by bending the bottoms of two hangers in half to hold each end of the dowel, then hooking the hangers on top of door, fixture, or whatever is available. For portability, she ties many cords in bundles *(below)*. Only the portions she's working on are unwrapped at the time.

a. Grasp several lengths and make an overhand knot over your wrist.
b. Reach through and grasp the cords below the knot.
c. Pull through the loop leaving your hand in this loop. Grasp the cords again below that loop until the cords resemble a hand-crocheted chain *(above)*. Cords will be tied out of the way until needed.

a.

b.

c.

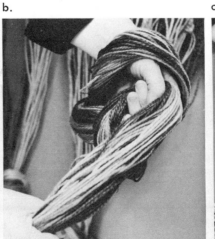

Organized working methods will minimize the tedious aspects of Macramé and allow more time for creativity. Joan Paque keeps spools of twine and yarn on a warping or bobbin rack which has dowels that lift out. Spools may be unwound directly from the core which twirls on the dowel. She also can see her assortment at a glance.

A weaver's warping rack is a convenient device for measuring a number of threads without tangling, or for improvising ways to measure efficiently. Wind cords around door or drawer handles. Hammer spikes into a working area and wind cords around these.

a length of cord will have a slub, knot, or other imperfection that requires excising and reattaching.

It is not unusual to hear someone say that Macramé is such a pure form of knotting that a piece is ruined if cord or glue must be added. From a creative approach, such thinking is passé. It's the finished result that counts, regardless of the route one takes to achieve it.

There also are several suggestions for the use and preparations of beads and other added items—an important adjunct to knotting.

Finding unusual materials and combinations of materials is part of the challenge of knotting. In addition to cords, already discussed,

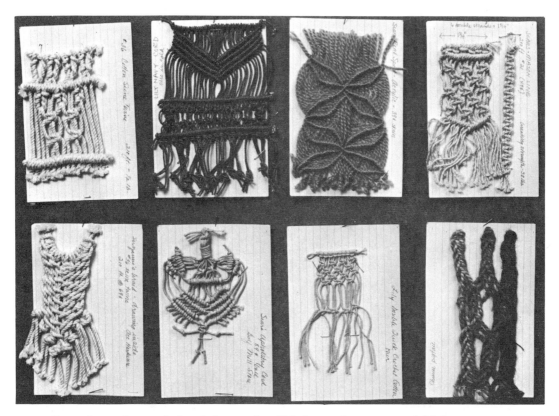

Knotted samples stapled to index cards will help you keep a record of the type of cord, where available, and price. It can also serve as a "measure" of the number of cords per inch required for knotting that particular cord: see card upper right. Dorris Akers also uses cards as samples of knots and their appearance in specific patterns and cords.

Yarn and cord sample cards may be referred to quickly if they are in a notebook or in some other easily accessible, organized filing system.

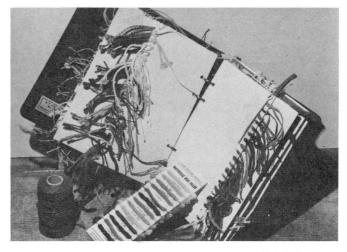

YELLOW NECKLACE. Marci Zelmanoff. Fine 24-gauge silver wire
with yellow linen. The wire is a
support for Clove Hitches in linen.
It is also knotted in some areas.
Courtesy, artist

knotting may be done with plastic, leather, or wire.

Some handling problems of materials have been solved by individual
knotters. When you wish to mix yarn colors, wind four of five skeins of
different hues into one ball. Pull knotting lengths from the balls
all together so the hues are treated as one length of cord.

If cords do not hold a desired shape, they may be stiffened by in-
corporating wire into the knotting. Wire may be introduced as a
horizontal bar with Clove Hitching over it. Fine wire, a brazing bar,
or curtain rod might be used depending on the cord and stiffening
required. Shapes also may be stiffened by putting white emulsion glue
(Elmer's, Sobo) onto the cord, then supporting the shape or placing
it on a piece of waxed paper until glue sets. Several applications
of spray starch will also stiffen some knotting.

If cord ends twist and curl, weight them from behind by tying on
stones or metal washers. These may be wound with the same cord,
then knotted or stitched to the backing so they won't show.

PLASTIC HANGING. Mary Baughn. Clear plastic strips, 8' long, 2' wide. An unusual adaptation of materials to Macramé in a successful, imaginative manner. Areas are woven in addition to knotting.

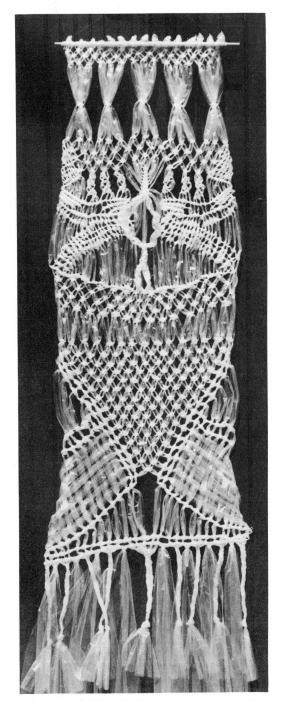

FREE-FORM HANGING. Lynn Doran. Suede strips and linen yarn, 44" long, 7" diameter. One large suede hide was cut into strips, leaving a solid, uncut section at top. This was cut, shaped, and stitched as a solid form with the strips hanging from it. Some strips were pulled to the center, combined with linen, then knotted. The remainder of the strips became an outer layer creating a solid inner core with an open linear form around it.

Jute, sisal, hemp, and any other roughly textured cords often are hard on the fingers when tying and pulling cords. Wear gloves or use Band-Aids across fingers most used in tying.

Nylon and other synthetic slick, slippery cords tend to fray at the ends while working. Singe with a match to melt the ends and prevent the plies from untwisting. Do a burn test on a small sample first. Burning is also a test for determining a cord's content. Silk or cotton will burn rather than melt as nylon does.

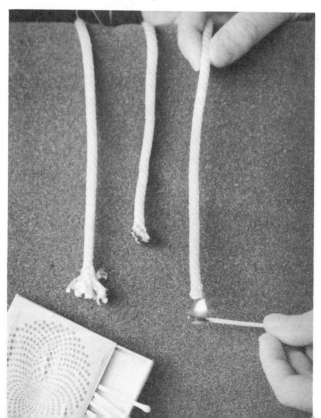

COLOR AND CORDS

Color is an exciting aspect of Macramé. Unfortunately, not so exciting is the range of color available in textured, thick cords so marvelous for large, sculptural work. Color is available in lightweight jutes and yarns, but if one wishes to go color happy with heavier material, it is almost essential to dye cords yourself.

Use any fabric and textile dye such as Cushing's, Rit and Tintex, batik dyes, or India ink. Cords may be dyed before tying, but care must be taken to prevent tangling. They should be loosely wound in skeins, then carefully dipped in dye solution. One can dye a tied piece if it will fit into a container. Always test-dye a sample fiber before dying an entire batch of cord or a finished piece.

Some knotters paint dye solutions on cords if they want special colorations in isolated areas or if dyes have not penetrated the material, but these may rub off eventually.

For hangings or jewelry that will be washed, dyes should be colorfast. Dyes not boiled may be set by adding up to a cup of vinegar per package to the dye solution. Dyed textiles might be pretested for sun fading if they will be sold as colorfast. Some knotters preshrink all cotton cords before tying.

HANGING. Joan Michaels Paque. Jute-tone. 36" wide, 20" high.
Photographed at Art Independent, Lake Geneva, Wisconsin

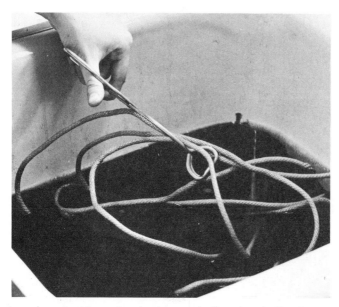

Lengths of white nylon braid are being tinted. For larger quantities, wrap cords loosely into skeins, tie at top and bottom, and drop into dye. Watch the color absorption for hue intensity. In cold-water dyes, fading can be prevented by adding vinegar to dye solution. Try "tie-dying" techniques for variegated colors. Tint sufficient cords for one piece of work so dye lots do not vary.

A finished piece of cotton seine twine jewelry is dyed complete with wood beads. Beads and cord absorb dye for an overall pastel tone. Sometimes dye does not penetrate the knots completely and this may be considered part of the beauty of the piece. Experimentation will result in unlimited effects.

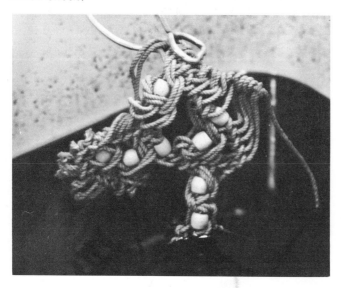

When working with multiple colors, it is often difficult to determine where some colors will end up as the knotting progresses. Utilize the happenstance of color as a creative aspect of Macramé too. With experience you'll learn to control colors in given areas.

Work in progress by Antonette Pattullo

WEAVING AND MACRAMÉ. Corki Weeks. Color may be carefully planned and controlled by adding cords or by combining color with weaving and Macramé.

ADDING CORDS

Often you will want to add cords to your work: when one or more cords become too short for knotting, when you want to expand or increase a section, or when you wish to add a color. Much will depend on the kind of cord you're using and whether or not you wish the addition to show. For nonvisible additions, splicing the cord is most satisfactory. This is done by unraveling both ends to be joined, dipping or rubbing them in a fabric cement, then simply twisting the ends together. Allow the joint to dry thoroughly before using any "pull" pressure. A waterproof rubber cream cement has proved excellent for the purpose, and the glued joint does not become stiff. Try other fabric glues also.

Another nonvisible method for adding to a short cord or introducing a color is to place a T pin behind the work where the new cord is to be added. Tie the new cord to the pin as though it was a horizontal line and simply work it into the knotting. Ends may be glued or woven in by hand or needle later.

If fringes and ends are a part of the surface texture of the work, permit added loose ends to hang, possibly accentuating the lengths, and knot the cords in where necessary. Adding cords is so feasible that you can begin with one cord and add 500 if desired.

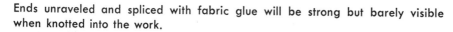

Ends unraveled and spliced with fabric glue will be strong but barely visible when knotted into the work.

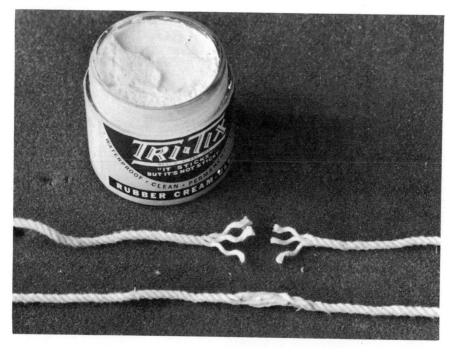

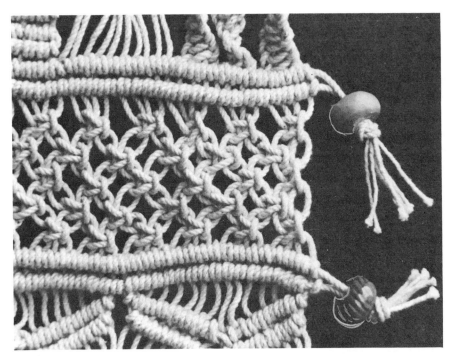

Beads may be tied to the ends for greater interest. Also, try using single, double, even triple lengths of cord to tie in for bars if thicker horizontals will enhance the composition.

Horizontal anchor bars use up more cord than the vertical lengths. Rather than use right and left end cords, add new lengths of cords, wood dowels, metal rods, etc., as horizontal anchor bars. The piece may purposely be made more decorative with these additions. Ends may be knotted or camouflaged into the row from behind.

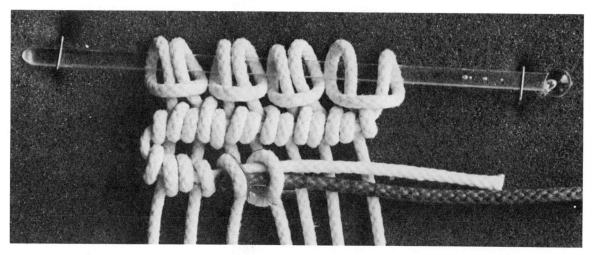

An easy way to add a cord that may have been underestimated, or to work in a new color, is to add it to a horizontal bar.

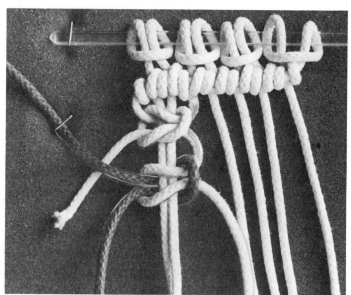

a

b

Cords are added easily between the anchor cords of a Square Knot or in any kind of chains utilizing anchor cords.

a. New cord added between anchors of Square Knot. To increase, mount four new Square Knotting cords between tied Square Knots using the loops of the adjacent Square Knots to pull new cords through.

b. New cord added as a knotting cord.

c. New cord added on a vertical with a Lark's Head.

c

DETAIL. Neda Al-Hilali. In free assymmetrical works, when ends and fringed textures often are part of the expressiveness of the piece, cords may be added almost anywhere. Thick and thin bars are a natural place to add new colors and varied materials.

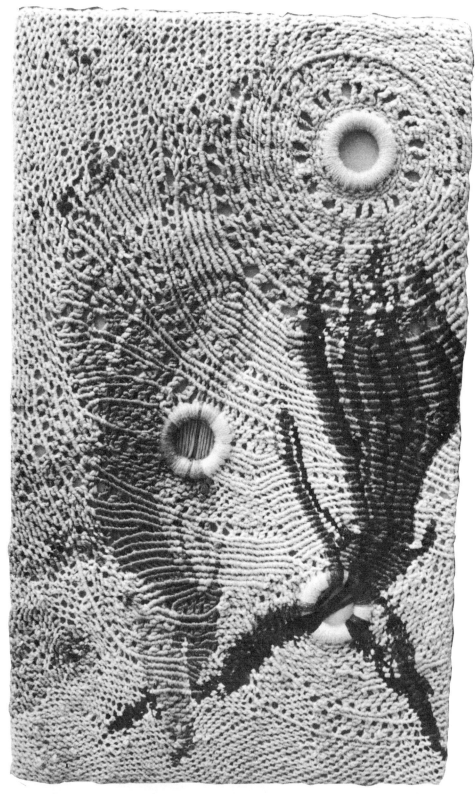

SEA FORMS. Marion Smith Ferri. Composition in yarns stretched over a board, then mounted on a panel of wood: 30" high, 22" wide. An obvious example of color added along the rows of Clove Hitches. To drop colors, simply leave them out at the back or wind two cords at a time until they taper off.

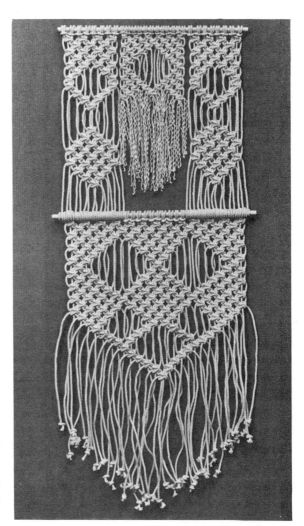

HANGING. Dorris Akers. #72 white cotton seine twine, 36″ long, 15″ wide. The central cords were cut and frazzled in the top center; new cords were mounted on the center of the horizontal dowel bar to continue the negative-positive diamond pattern.

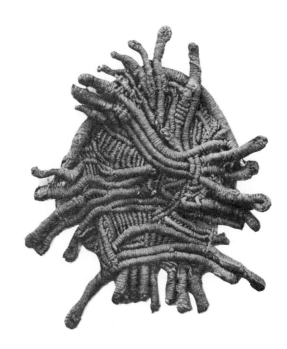

ORGANIC FORM. Judy Kinnell. Dyed hemp, 15″ high, 13″ wide. Thick and thin forms interpenetrate in this richly textured piece done completely in Clove Hitches. To create the varying sized bars, it was essential to add cords.

ADDING BEADS AND OTHER THINGS

Beads are an important Macramé adjunct. They provide a surface enrichment compatible with the raised knot shapes and a relief to straight knotting. One problem is to find interesting beads with holes large enough to accommodate double, triple, and more cords required for knotting. There are several ways to overcome the bead problem. Some suppliers are beginning to create beads with large holes. If these are not available, buy strung Indian beads, Hippie beads, or bamboo curtain beads and cut them apart. You can easily create your own ceramic and papier-mâché beads. When bead holes offer resistance to threading, use a fine wire for stringing or dip the ends of the cords into melted wax, shape the ends to a point, and let the wax harden to make stringing easier.

Other items often used with knotting are shells, buttons, bells, medallions, coins, plastic straws cut to lengths, copper and brass tubing and springs available in hardware stores.

Trees and plants yield interesting forms usable in Macramé. The dried cactus root has a triangular negative pattern ideal for mounting cords. Seed pods, hard-shell nuts, meat bones, and feathers are among the varied items you will observe in examples throughout the book.

Assorted natural and man-made items used for stringing on Macramé. Highly glazed ceramic beads have holes large enough for Macramé. Wood and glass beads are bought as necklaces, then unstrung and reused. Pods from a tree are dried, the stems left intact and wrapped into the work rather than strung.

Instant papier-mâché and self-hardening ceramic clay (which requires no kiln firing) are readily made into marvelous lightweight beads that may be individually colored. Form them around a plastic malted milk straw so a large hole is provided for stringing. Hand or spray paint. For a high gloss, spray with a clear varnish or acrylic. Novel spray finishes such as pearl tones, leather texture, golds and silvers are available, too.

When holes of beads and other items are too small for stringing or no hole exists, use a hand drill. Holes may be drilled in wood strips, driftwood, and branches to use for unusual mounting bars. Bars need not be perfectly straight; often odd shapes are interesting for mounting.

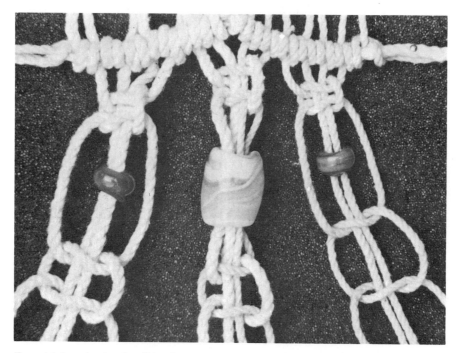

To add beads simply slide them on your cords between or in the middle of knots. Add beads to cords before winding butterflies, then slip the beads up as needed as though working an abacus. No need to unwrap butterflies. When bead holes are too small for cords they may be wired to the cord.

NECKLACES. Virginia Black. Yarn, seashells, and sea anemones make unusual pieces of one-of-a-kind jewelry.

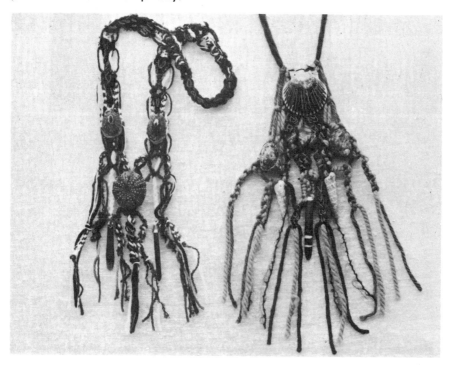

NECKLACES. Eileen Bernard. Assorted wood beads, bells, chains are used in various places along the jewelry. Notice the unusual mounting lines made of metal which has been heated and shaped into coils. Mrs. Bernard's jewelry often is inspired by details from African native costumes.

HANGING. Eileen Bernard. Jute, 29" high, 13" wide. Illustrates unusual mechanics of mounting and the use of found objects, rings, and wrought iron.

FETISH. Margaret Roth. A potpourri of objects with Macramé and free crochet. Top was a hand broom. Feathers, plastic wood and natural clay beads, bones, seeds, and a bell are attached and incorporated into the piece.

Photographed at Design West, California

Detail of Eileen Bernard's piece *(left)*. Mounting is on rings in two directions with Lark's Head. Top section is worked and bar added with Clove Hitches; the remaining ends brought to the front and made into tassels. At lower horizontal bar, cords are added for continuing design.

Detail of Fetish *(left)* showing the addition of feathers and beads.

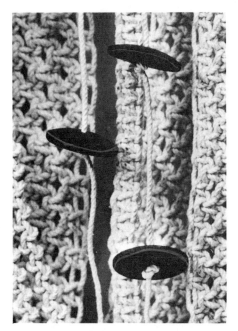

Wood discs sold for craft decor have had holes drilled and been colored with India ink. They are held in place with an Overhand Knot at bottom.

HANGING (detail). Stana Coleman. Four ➤ rows of black and white wood beads strung on wire for round shape. Cords added at bottom row for knotting.

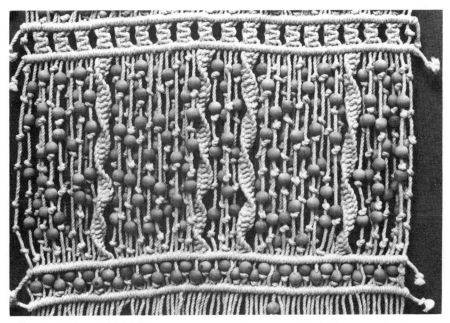

Natural wood beads add a surface treatment for texture and design. All are held in place with the Overhand Knot which also forms part of the design.

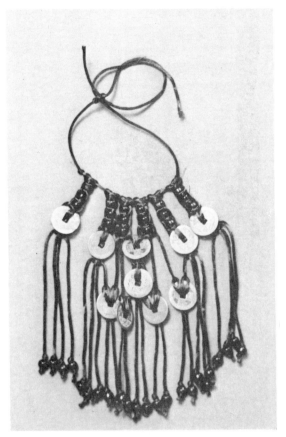

NECKLACE. Stana Coleman. Silk rattail cord sold for hat and drapery trim knotted with beads and antique coins.

NECKLACE. Stana Coleman. Linen cord of Half Knot twist. Copper-color beads and copper tubing from hardware store.

NECKLACE. Joan Michaels Paque. White jute with buttons worked into unusual design.

Photographed at Art International, Lake Geneva, Wisconsin

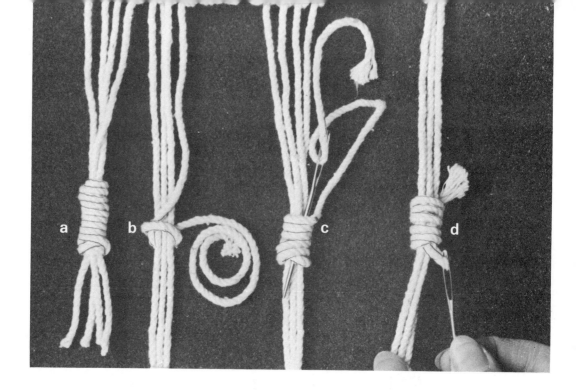

WHAT TO DO WITH ENDS

Ending a knotted project often presents problems. The solutions may be found most readily by studying examples throughout this book. Wrapping, illustrated above, is an efficient, solid way of ending a series of loose cords. It may be done with one of the cords already on the piece, or another color or texture may be introduced.

Other techniques include a row of beads held with an Overhand Knot; a series of Overhand Knots, only a knot at the bottom; the alternating Half Hitch (described on page 135), fringing and fraying the cord by unraveling its plies.

Ends may be braided with three or more cords and held with an Overhand Knot. Twist two or more sets of cords in a clockwise direction, then twist the groups together in a counterclockwise direction. Tie an Overhand Knot to hold the twists together. For a gnarled effect twist the cord in the same direction as its original twist until it bends up in odd shapes.

A series of Monkey's Fist Knots (page 160) may be used. For a solid end without any dangling cords, Clove Hitch over a horizontal bar, then bring the ends up to the back of the work and weave them into the knots. Ends may be glued or stitched for better holding. The back may be faced with a piece of fabric to hold the ends—particularly for clothes, purses, and accessories that will be handled a great deal.

Tassels, long and short, are decorative and functional. They may be made with the Macramé heading (page 166) or bundled and wrapped.

◄ WRAPPING A COIL

  a. Finished wrapped coil using one of four cords to wrap. Any multiples may
   be used.
  b. With end of one cord begin wrapping at *bottom* of coil. Overlap first wrap
   to prevent coil from slipping and continue winding.
  c. Wrap large-eye needle into coil with eye at top. At end of number of wraps
   desired, thread loose end through needle.
  d. Pull needle through all the wraps to the bottom. Tighten coil by twisting
   gently. Cut ends to even lengths if desired.

Cords may be wrapped from top to bottom and loose end pulled from bottom
to top of cord and cut and glued.

For cords that are too thick to thread through a needle, wrap loosely and push
the end back down through the wraps. Tighten.

Another way to wrap is to mount a doubled cord with a Lark's Head to the
group of strands to be wrapped. Continue to wrap both strands of the added
cord around the group. Slip ends of cord up through last two wraps, snip close.
Glue to hold.

An Overhand Wrap may also be used to finish ends. The number of wraps is
determined by the number of times the end is wound around the loop.

To create the wrap, make a large loop. Fold one end back and make several
winds over the top of the loop. Pull both ends gently until coil forms.

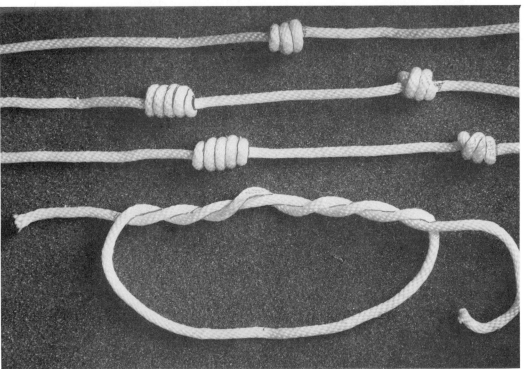

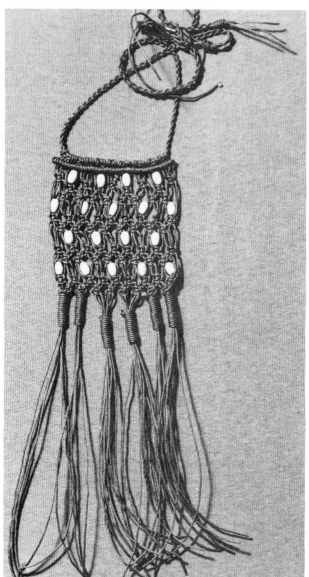

NECKLACE. Sally Davidson. Gray linen
with wrapped ends. Observe that wrapping is at different heights on the cords.

Detail showing different endings from ➤
a Clove Hitched chevron. Beads are
held with Half Knots and many cords
unraveled.

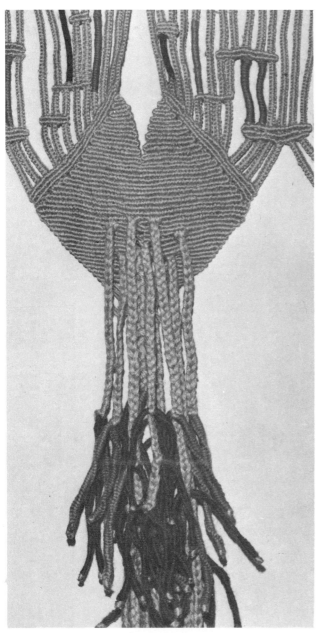

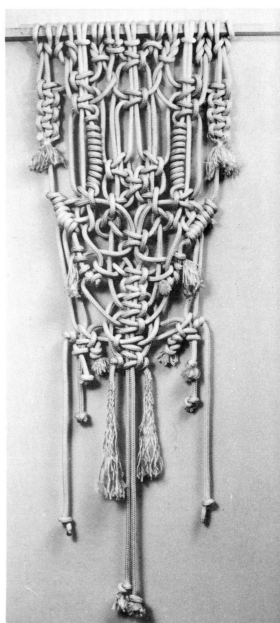

BLUE AND PURPLE (detail). Michi Ouchi. Endings braided and Clove Hitch Chains (Chapter 6) added in varying colors. Chains are wrapped at ends. Observe wrapping used in body of piece also.
Courtesy, Michi Ouchi

HANGING. Dorris Akers. ½″ diameter nylon yacht braid, 48″ long, 18″ wide. Various techniques for ending are employed. Near center bottom, Square Knots are anchored with Overhand Knots: ends are slightly unbraided at first, then cascade into a completely unbraided fringe. Short frayed ends are used in some areas, in others, an Overhand Knot is finished by singeing the end to melt it and prevent fraying.

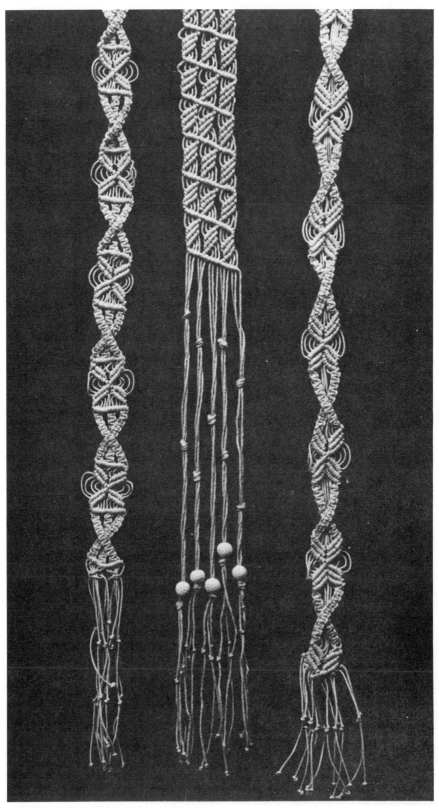

BELTS. Sarajane Bitterman. White seine twine. More variations for endings. Center belt utilizes handmade ceramic beads.

JEWEL OF THE SEA. Else Regensteiner. 64" high, 36" wide. When multiple cords are used, the almost haphazard placement of cords in a rich variety of texture, colors, and hues, held together with a Square Knot Chain, is simple and exciting.

Photo, John W. Rosenthal

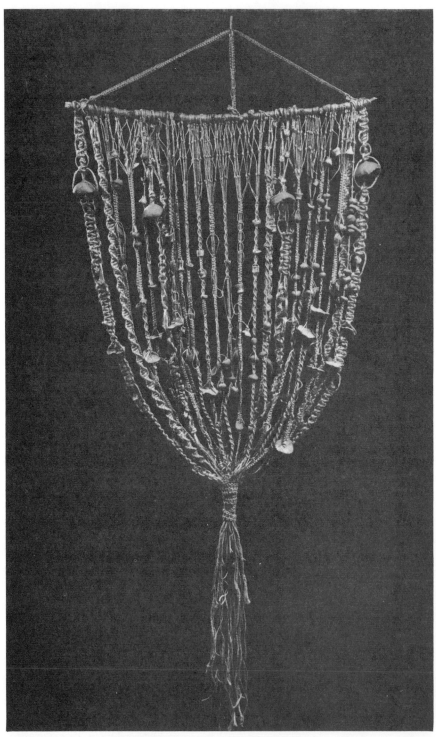

SIAM. Else Regensteiner. Assorted cords with ceramic discs, 45" high, 25" wide.
Idea stimulated by banners seen during a trip to Siam.

Photo, John W. Rosenthal

4

Sources and Ideas for Macramé Forms and Designs

Once you have mastered the knots, the real excitement of Macramé lies in the forms and dimensions you can evolve. Tying knots for their own sake can become monotonous, but the infinite forms, shapes, and designs possible with them are the challenge and fascination.

To help you discover potential design ideas, it is important to train your eye and mind to recognize possible sources for details and entire pieces. Every artist cultivates this awareness. The beauty and detail in one petal of a rose, for example, may have a more dramatic impact for artistic interpretation than the entire flower. The natural design of a butterfly's wing is so intricately patterned, it offers more ideas than the whole butterfly. Such awareness of detail can stimulate exciting knotting ideas.

On the following pages, objects are shown that could possibly have stimulated the design of the accompanying Macramé pieces. The same objects could be interpreted in a hundred different ways by a hundred knotters. The correlations are presented to help you observe and relate what you see to your work.

In addition to the items shown, consider the following for knotting motifs: Arabic and Oriental calligraphy, medieval and Renaissance illuminated manuscript borders, art nouveau swirls and patterns, details from stone carving or ironwork. Tiffany glassware patterns, architectural shapes, Polynesian, Indian, and Aztec designs, wickerwork, rose windows, Arabic mosaics, barbed wire fences, contemporary and Oriental fabrics, and impressions from your travels.

HANGING. Neva Humphreys. Sisal, 42" long, 26" wide. The knotted cords at the top are given rigidity by being sewn to a metal hook covered with hem binding. The design might have been inspired by an artistic eye that has learned to take the obvious and interpret it in a personal way. Below, a blossom, seen upside down, may spark a similar form for Macramé.

From nature, the list of idea sources is endless. Flowers, root formations, swirls of tree knots, microscopic details from photos of cells, patterns in slices of fruits and vegetables, colors from birds, etc.

With observation and practice, you'll learn to cull from various visual notes the types of things applicable to knotting. You may be amazed at how easy it is to adapt designs from things you have consciously observed for the purpose.

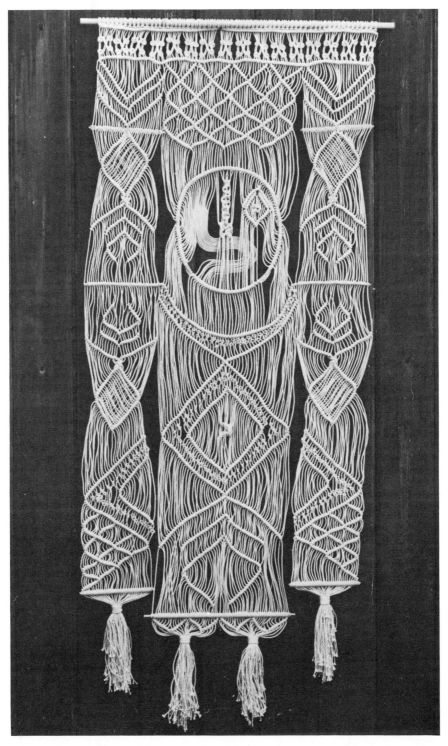

THE WHITE GODDESS. Sibyl Pritchard. White seine twine, 56″ long, 24″ wide. A personal symbolic iconography provided the design concept. A technical aspect of this piece is that the curved cords in the central ring are stiffened with a piece of gummed paper cut to the shape desired. The central circle, horizontal bar and semicircle are metal so the piece will retain its shape.

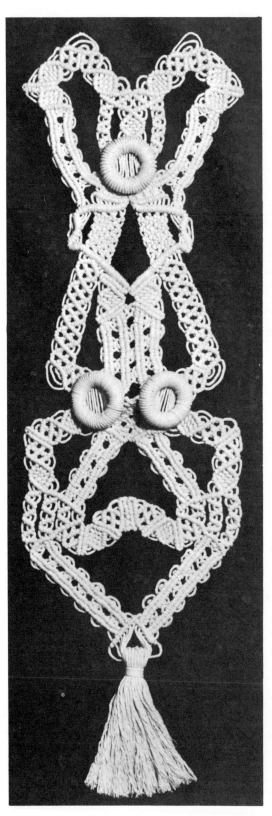

OMEGA. Joan Michaels Paque. Cotton twine with wood drapery rings covered by Clove Hitching and attached.

Photo, Henry Paque

HANGING ON LUCITE. Marion Smith Ferri. 30" long, 16" wide. Large areas of floating cords combined with tightly controlled knotting patterns.

Stone Gate, Greece, might have served as the inspiration for Joan Paque's "Omega" left. Select only a few of the curves and swirls for a small piece of jewelry. Or use parts of it for an entire piece of flat Macramé.

Photo, Mel Meilach

Wrought Iron door has the same feeling as the lucite hanging, left. Large areas of straight iron are combined with tightly patterned areas in the same relationship as Mrs. Ferri's floating and knotted cords.

ALUPHIAN. Imelda Pesch. Natural sisal wool cotton and rayon rug yarns. Macramé with some weaving and hooking. The title means "masklike."

Courtesy, artist

MASK. Ambryn Island, New Hebrides. Hemp, fibers bark, and traces of color show the use of materials and shapes by primitive man that can stimulate ideas for Macramé.

Courtesy, Art Institute of Chicago

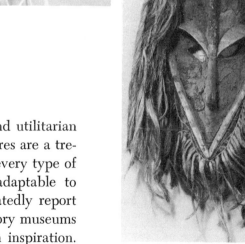

The dress, ceremonial, and utilitarian objects of primitive cultures are a tremendous inspiration for every type of artwork and especially adaptable to Macramé. Knotters repeatedly report that visits to natural history museums are invaluable for design inspiration.

IBO. Libby Crawford. Waxed
upholsterer's cord, 17" high,
4" wide.

Courtesy, artist

CEREMONIAL SHIELD. Mary
Sue Foster. Jute and sisal. 5'
high, 3' wide.

Courtesy, artist

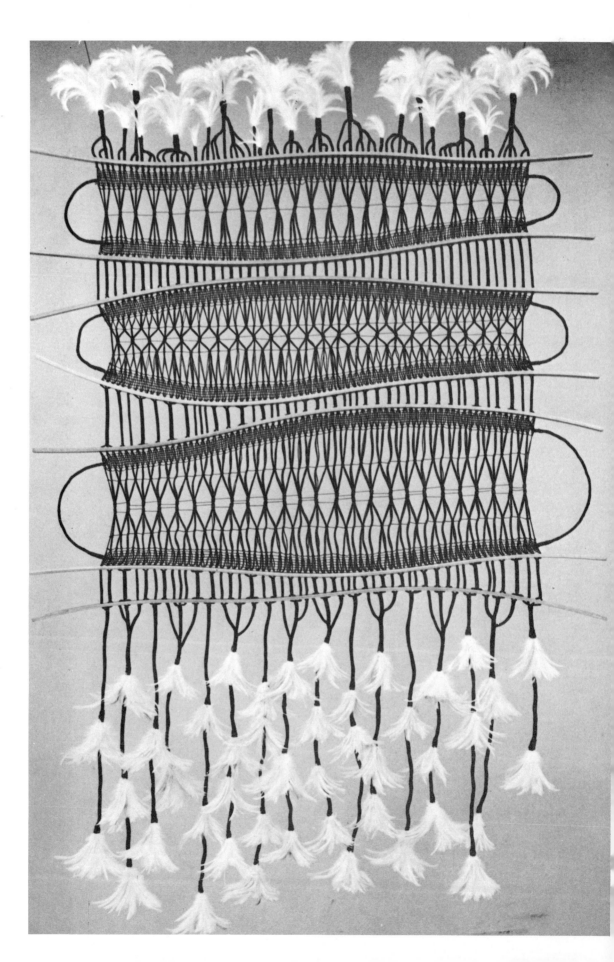

◄ MACRAMÉ HANGING. John Snidecor.
Cotton fishing twine dyed black, 6' high,
4' wide. String was coated with bees-
wax to make wrapping easier. Horizontal slats are laminated white oak.
Chicken feathers wound in give the
hanging a primitive feeling.

Courtesy, artist

PRIMITIF. Rosita Montgomery. Black
horsehair, natural jute, guinea hen
feathers, Indian brass bells and pre-
Columbian beads, 36" high, 10" wide.

Collection, Mrs. Lester Barnes, Perryton, Texas
Photo, Lee Payne

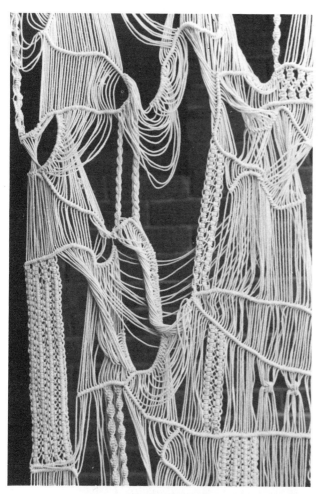

COMPOSITION IN WHITE V (detail).
Estelle Carlson. Carpenter's chalk line.
The crossovers, negative and positive
areas, and organic feeling of this hanging could easily be related to root
formations (below).

Courtesy, artist

HOMAGE TO GAUDI. Aurelia Muñoz.
White cotton cord. This sculptural Macramé motif was inspired by the architectural forms of Antonio Gaudi's build-
ings in Barcelona, Spain.

Courtesy, Galeria Juana Mordo, Madrid

An entire church steeple can provide
design ideas in either two- or three-
dimensional statements. Select small
portions of the stone or ironwork and
use for patterns, too.

Photo, Mel Meilach

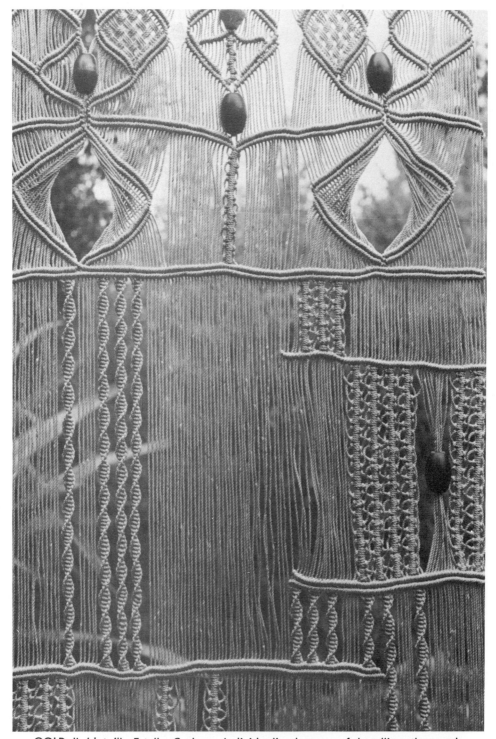

GOLD II (detail). Estelle Carlson. Individualized ways of handling the cords have been developed by the artist through experience and experimentation. Notice how closely these details repeat the shapes and patterns of the objects at right.

Courtesy, artist

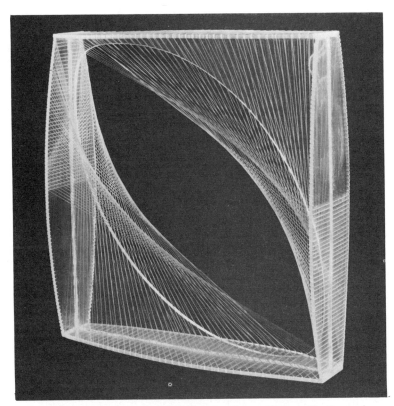

LINEAR CONSTRUCTION NO. 1. Naum Gabo. Plastic and nylon sculpture. Approximately 12" square.

Courtesy, Marlborough Fine Art Ltd., London

Broken areas of a barbed wire fence possess a space relationship similar to those in Estelle Carlson's Gold II, left.

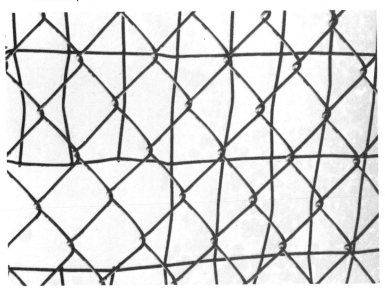

SCULPTURAL KNOTTING

"I simply worked shapes and patterns beginning at the top and 'adding various cords. I had no special ideas when I began," said the artist. However, a Thai dancer's headdress could have inspired such a shape.

Thai dancing doll headdress.

Collection, Dona Meilach

NINGIZZIDA. Estelle Carlson. Nylon twine, gold and white, 55" high, 24" wide. Verticals, horizontals, sweeps, and curves similar to these may be found in carved draperies of Indian and Greek stone sculptures.

Courtesy, artist

Detail of drapery from a Buddha can be a source of ideas for draping cords in unusual ways.

SPACE HANGING (detail). Gloria Crouse. Narrow and swelling shapes may have their origin in the natural rock formation *(below)*. The artist is free to use portions of any object consciously or sub-consciously. He can repeat or depart from any detail into any creative direction.

Photo, Mary Sue Foster

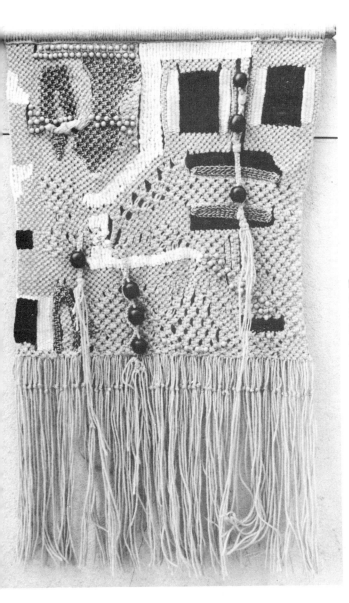

HANGING. Marion Smith Ferri. In this small, colorful piece one can find shapes associated with architectural detail. The windows, the descending oblique staircase and the horizontal railing of the Greek church (below) have their counterparts in the hanging.

RED FOREST. Claire Zeisler. Dyed jute, 8' high with base. A sculpture composed of Square Knotted forms is suspended from a ceiling with the strands carefully spread at its base.

Collection, First National Bank of Chicago
Photo, Jonas Dovydenas

5

Sculptural Macramé

Sculptural form in Macramé is an exciting development of twentieth-century textile art and a portent of the future. The potential sturdiness of multiple heavy cords knotted around an armature or self-supporting is unique to the art. With no tools or looms required, the size and range of shapes are infinite.

Developing a sculptural form is an experimental process with each piece presenting its own problems. Methods used to begin a three-dimensional piece are shown as a springboard to help you get the feeling of how really simple it is to work in-the-round and in free-form shapes.

By mounting cords on a hoop such as a plastic hula toy, a bicycle wheel, an embroidery ring, a circle of rattan, a welded wire—anything circular—you are immediately forced to think in terms of a piece that must be worked and viewed from more than one side. The piece occupies space and has space within. When suspended from a ceiling it will cast a shadow that must be thought of in relation to the piece itself.

An innovator of the "sculptured knot," as it was referred to in *Crafts Horizon Magazine,* is Claire Zeisler, who has carried knotting to an unprecedented statement, simple, yet monumental and a complete departure from traditional Macramé. Her free-standing pieces have no armature other than bound fibers. Joan Michaels Paque also achieves a monumental, architectural quality in her hangings that rely on a skeletal wire armature for their foundation. Gloria Crouse's statements rely on the use of unconventional materials such as leather and suede in addition to three-dimensional controlled geometric forms.

The idea of building on a natural form and repeating it in Macramé has been uniquely achieved by Libby Platus who so effectively combines many materials in her pieces.

INTROSPECTION. Joan Michaels Paque. White nylon seine twine over a wire armature, 9' high. Convex and concave shapes move in and out of the sculpture. The vertical wires are knotted over and held in tension by the horizontal hoops. Very loose knotting results in an airy composition that both exists in space and utilizes space within the volume.

Photo, Henry Paque

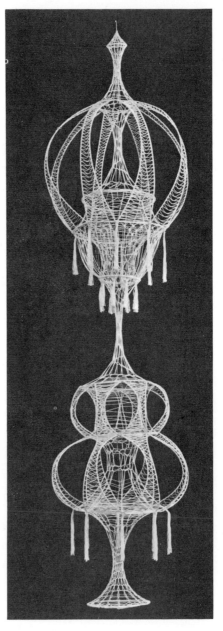

SPATIAL COLONNADE. Joan Michaels Paque. Jute dyed gold, orange, and red, 8' high. Series of metal hoops of varying diameter are tied into the knotting. Alternate Square Knots and floating cords give the tight-to-free knotting contrast. The decorative motif, center and near bottom, is a variation of a Clove Hitch Chain (Chapter 6) with beads added. Unraveled cords wrapped in tassels finish the piece.

Photo, Henry Paque

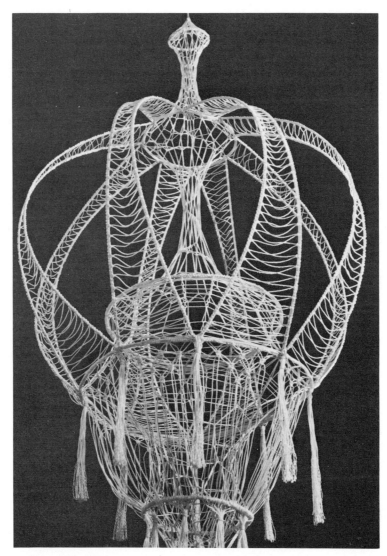

INTROSPECTION (detail). Joan Michaels Paque. Illustrates the simple knotting and the interior and exterior framework.

Photo, Henry Paque

Museum curators are beginning to recognize the importance of sculptural textiles, and many of the artists represented have already had pieces purchased for major collections and exhibits.

In the examples that follow, knots already learned usually are employed: the application is new. These artists have had no precedent, no examples of work by other knotters. They have set up a problem and solved it, thus creating an innovative, esthetic statement.

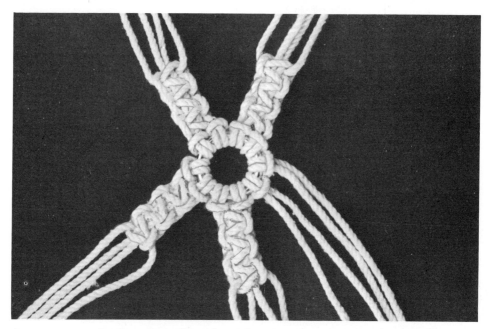

An easy way to begin a three-dimensional form is to mount cords on a circular ring—any size. Here a brass drapery rod ring is used for the center. Mount the usual multiples of four cords. You could also pin a cord in a circle and mount on that, but it won't be as stiff.

Then, tie in another ring a little larger with Clove Hitches. Because of the larger circumference of this second ring (an embroidery hoop) more cords may be added with a Lark's Head or hitched on for additional knotting. Larger hoops may be added indefinitely. For an "inner circle" of knotting, use about eight cords to tie in a smaller interior ring. Add cords on this inner ring and you are set up to knot on two levels.

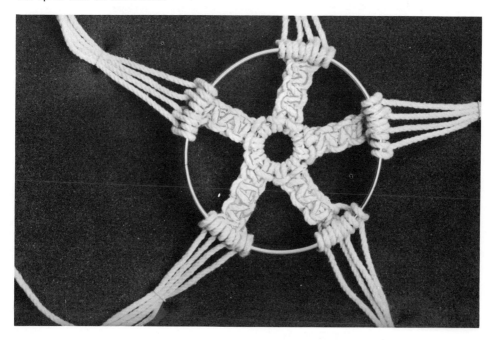

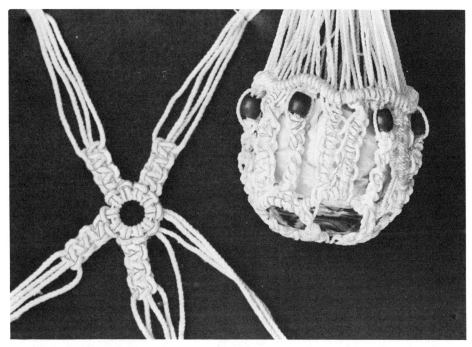

Here only the drapery ring center was used, then a second cord, rather than a hard loop, pinned to the board in a circle. The knotting was continued to form a decorative hanging for a pot, glass, or vase.

A wood ring is only partially covered with cords and its shape and color will be repeated and be part of the design.

A large hoop may support a relief portion of a knotting in this manner. Mikael
C. Carstenjen.

Interior form knotted tightly from a top
hoop. Some cords were used to attach
a second hoop around the outer circumference instead of knotting.

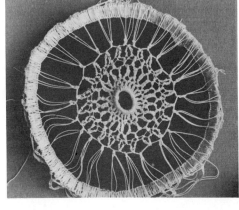

Beginning from a stiff rubber washer, the knotting continues outward where a rattan hoop is knotted in, then more cords added.

Drawing for hanging.

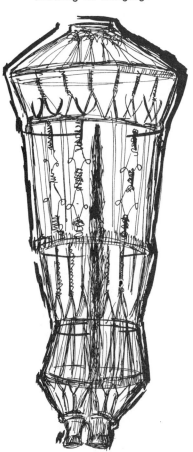

HANGING. Mary Geimer. White nylon seine twine, 6′ high, 18″ diameter.

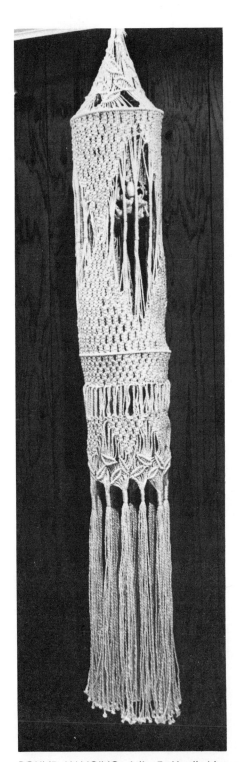

ROUND HANGING. Julia E. Littell. Natural jute, 6½' high. Hoops are those used for making Christmas wreaths. The piece was begun at the top wire hoop. Square Knots are made with four strands. Some cords dropped inside and half of these used for the inner center structure, other half brought up and made into leaf shapes at top. The center floating threads (see detail, right) were wrapped to reveal forms within.

BANNER ON A BEATER. Joyce Wexler. Yellow nylon twine mounted on an old-fashioned rug beater. 40″ long. All Square Knots and Half Knot Twists knotted at different levels. Unraveled ends hang loose.

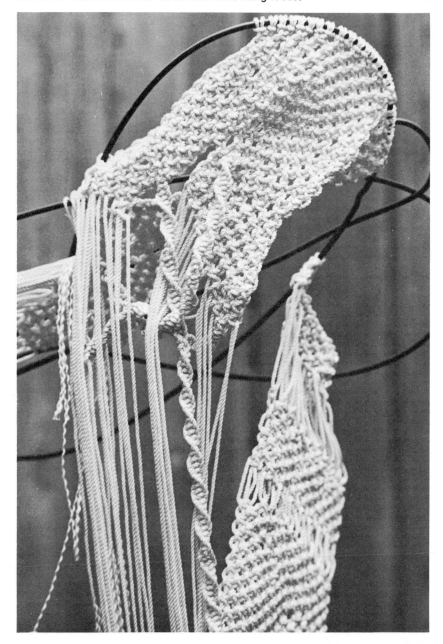

HANGING. Joy Lobell. Natural jute with black wrappings and beads, 54" long, 7" diameter. Wood hoops form the basic armature. Additional dimension achieved by using some of the cords for an exterior twist of Half Knot braids. The knotted jute becomes somewhat stiff by nature of the accumulation of cords.

Detail of double layer of knotting.

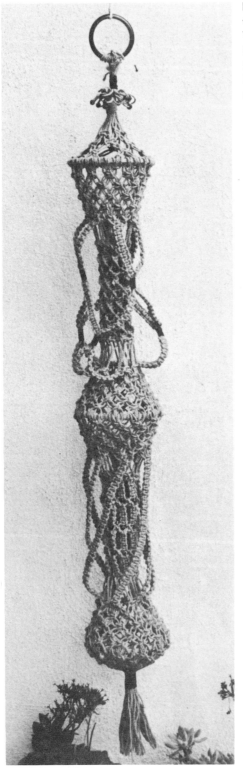

LEATHER AND MACRAMÉ. John Faulkner. 24″ high. Cords are mounted in holes of shaped and stitched leather pieces, then hoops knotted in and the Macramé is continued.

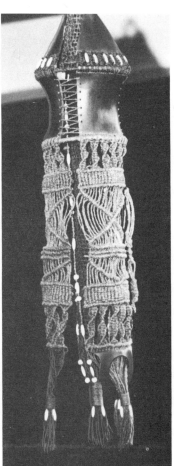

Detail of Suede Hanging (page 59). Lynn Doran. Suede stripped, leaving about eight inches to form a heading which has been cut, shaped, and sewn. This heading precludes three-dimensionality and becomes different from usual cord mountings. Knotting is done with the suede strips.

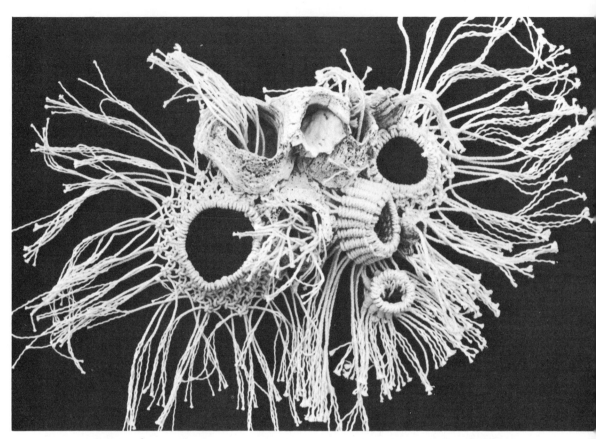

MACRAMÉ ON A BARNACLE. Libby Platus. White cotton seine twine, 20" high, 20" wide, 5" deep. Macramé knotted to repeat forms of barnacle shell and become one with it.

HANGING. Richard Frinier. Tarred hemp with teased jute tails, 3½' high, 1½' wide.

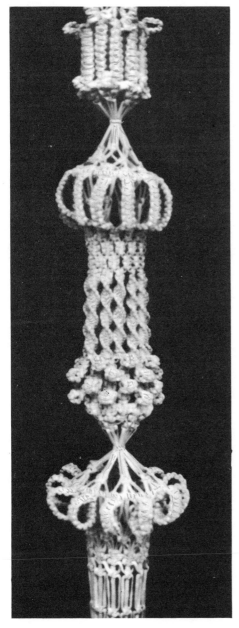

SPACE HANGING. Gloria Crouse. Beige cowhide, 7½' high, 6" diameter. Square Knot chains and Square Knot buttons (page 51) swell into space.
Photo, Mary Sue Foster

LLAP-SIDED LLAMA. Rosita Montgomery. Natural jute. 13″ high, 9″ long, 7″ wide. Horizontal and vertical Clove Hitches.

Photo, Lee Payne

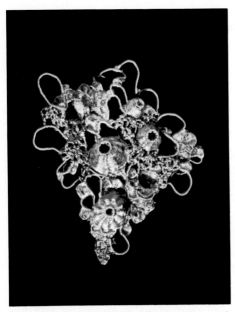

PENDANT. Marci Zelmanoff. Macramé with
silver wire, 6" x 7". *Courtesy, artist*

SUN HANGING. Esther Dendel. Macramé
and cardboard weaving, 48" x 26".
Photo, author

SCREEN. Joan Michaels Paque. Macramé set in
wood frame. *Photo, Henry Paque*

PONCHO. Edward Sherbeyn. Jute, red
wool, ceramic beads.
Courtesy, Edward Sherbeyn Gallery, Chicago

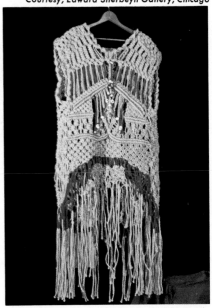

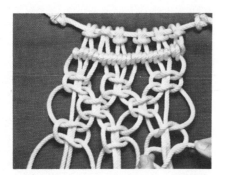

ALTERNATE SQUARE KNOT PATTERN.
Dona Meilach. Braided nylon cord.

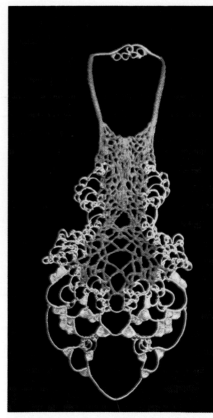

SILVER AND LINEN BIB. Marci Zelmanoff. 7" x 15". Square knots, wrapping, and knot variations.

Courtesy, artist

VALANCES. Joan Michaels Paque.

Photo, Henry Paque

WALL HANGING (detail). Joan Michaels Paque. *Photo, Henry Paque*

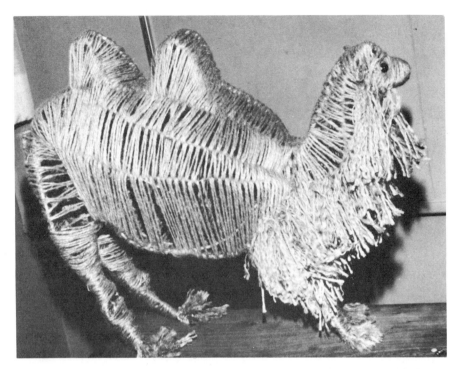

CAMEL. Mary Seramur. Natural jute wound and knotted over a welded wire armature.

Photo courtesy, Joan Michaels Paque

HIM. Louise Todd. Solidly knotted piece with beginning and end of cord at tail and mane. Some wrapping.

Courtesy, artist

MACRA-MOPS. Shirley Marein. Natural and dyed cotton mops on wire forms, 4½' to 6'. Shown on exhibition at the Museo de Las Culturas Internationale, Mexico City.

Photo, Juan Valdivia Aranda

BACK TO NATURE (detail). Michi Ouchi. Three-dimensional knotting forms are placed through a piece of fabric and stitched to it for still another use of Macramé as a relief shape from a flat surface.

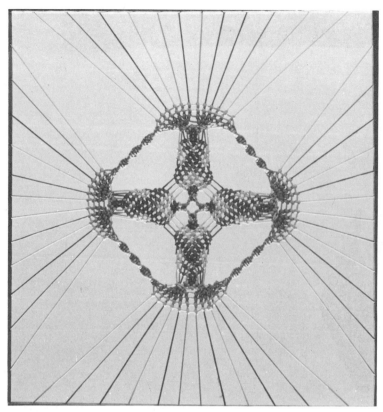

COMPOSITION: Peggy Wagner. Colored rattail mounted in a frame, 18" square. This piece was begun in the center with cords added as needed in an improvised manner. Loose ends stretched and knotted into wood frame with holes drilled.

CROSSOVER. Dorothy Smith. Nylon and jute are pulled through ready-made holes in an old chair seat once used for cane.

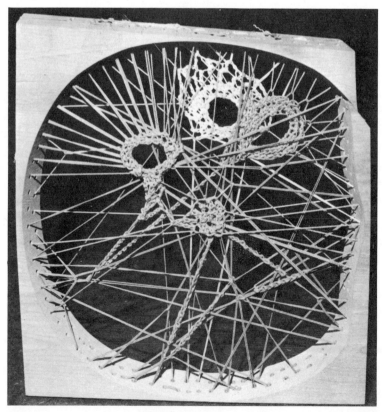

MACRAMÉ IN A DOORWAY. Peggy Wagner. Heavy jute, framed, about 30″ square. All Clove Hitches. This piece was startling hanging in the weathered old doorway of the artist's studio in Santa Fe.

Many weavers, already enchanted by the medium of natural fibers, are exploring form with Macramé. Claire Zeisler has parlayed this interest into rich, exciting architectonic pieces. Many of her sculptures are in major museum and private collections. This supports the trend to recognition of these new fiber forms as a serious expression by the serious artist.

Claire Zeisler's pieces are exquisitely simple, relying extensively on the single material, dyed jute (sometimes a softer yarn of wool is incorporated). Her pieces are uncluttered and large, as high as nine feet tall. The free-standing pieces have no metal armature or support; she established the problem of creating strength with fibers alone. The understructures utilize only wrapping and knotting for support while the myriad ends become part of the sculptural texture and form.

YELLOW PRESENCE (detail). Claire Zeisler. The understructure for the sculpture at right consists of wrapping many strands of the fibers for strength and support.

YELLOW PRESENCE. Claire Zeisler. Yellow jute with some black wool for wrapping, 5' high. Self-supporting, free-standing piece.

Collection, Mr. and Mrs. Abel Fagen, Lake Forest, Illinois
Photo, Jonas Dovydenas

Claire Zeisler develops a maquette, or sample, of a piece on a small scale, then graphs it for enlargement.

Because her pieces are so large and require so much handling, Claire Zeisler
has other craftsmen help her. For easier Square Knotting, note that the girl at
right has the anchor cords tied around her waist. At right of photo is a warping
board for measuring lengths of jute.

Photos, Jonas Dovydenas

RED WEDNESDAY. Claire Zeisler. Jute dyed, 66" high. A hanging piece that is the same on both sides.

Photo, Jonas Dovydenas

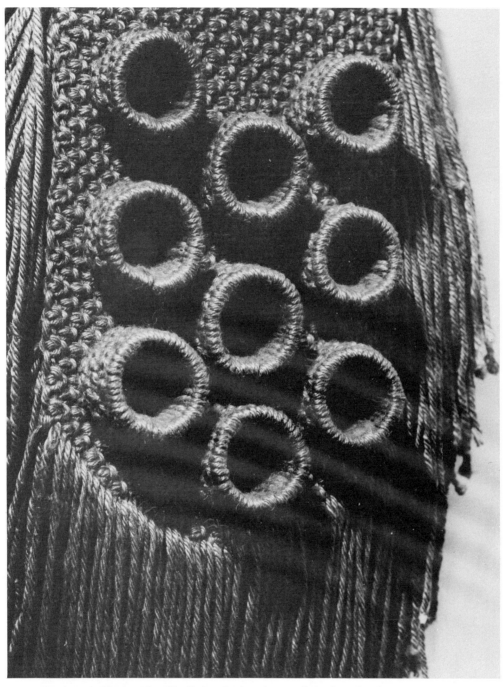

RED WEDNESDAY (detail). Claire Zeisler. Some of the knotting has been brought forward to create these sculptural cuplike forms. Ends have been carefully worked back into the cups.

Photo, Jonas Dovydenas

RED PREVIEW. Claire Zeisler. Jute dyed red. 6' high. A self-supporting wall piece. The wrappings and knotting are both structure and composition.

Photo, Jonas Dovydenas

SCULPTURES ON EXHIBITION at the Richard Feigen Gallery, Chicago, 1968.
Claire Zeisler.

Photo, Jonas Dovydenas

Variations of the Clove Hitch

6

The versatility and variations possible with the Clove Hitch are amazing. And fun. Following are more ideas for working the Clove Hitch around cords that are held in whatever angle or curve you wish the knots to take. By the time you have made several rows of Clove Hitches, you should be able to work out any pattern by simply looking at it. The following examples are offered to give you more ideas for using this knot and to lead you into new directions of your own.

In addition to the varied patterns one can make with the Clove Hitch, the knot also is formed into interesting chains (beginning on page 133) that are fascinating to do. Chains may be incorporated into hangings and used instead of or in conjunction with Square Knot sennits. They may be used individually for belts, neckbands, jewelry, headbands, and as a design motif in clothing.

Chain Clove Hitching does differ slightly from the Clove Hitch procedure you have already learned. For horizontal and diagonal Clove Hitching you always begin with the knotting cord *under* the anchor cord. For chains, you begin with the knotting cord *over* the anchor cord. For this reason, the knot is sometimes referred to as the "Reverse Half Hitch." However, the names of the knots themselves vary with different writers, and are not so important.

The Clove Hitch used in various patterns and combinations by Sarajane Bitterman for headbands. All cotton seine twine.

Left to right:

a. Detail of a diamond pattern.

b. Diamond pattern in groups of three bars. The cords have been pulled out to accentuate curves before knotting the next group of diagonal Clove Hitches.

c. Groups of four diagonal Clove Hitch bars. Observe that some are not tied in the middle; some central cords are tied with a Square Knot for added detail.

d. Clove Hitches with accentuated curves, horizontal bars, and Square Knot chains.

e. Clove Hitches made in leaf patterns.

f. Double diamond shapes with horizontal bars and short diagonal rows of Clove Hitches.

The leaf pattern in natural jute. To make a leaf, pick up vertical cord where you want the tip of the leaf to begin. Use it for an anchor cord and pin it in a slightly curving shape, then Clove Hitch eight or more vertical strands left to right. Reverse the anchor cord and hold in an opposing curve to create the desired leaf shape; Clove Hitch right to left. For the second row, pick up a vertical cord halfway along the first leaf to use for an anchor, and make another leaf shape in the desired direction. Detail from a hanging by Julia Littell.

Bear in mind, when doing variations, that the Clove Hitch actually is tied with two loops or Half Hitches. By reversing the direction of one of the loops, the appearance of the knot changes. Also, by placing the knotting cord *under* the anchor for the second loop, the Lark's Head can result for another knotting variation. These changes are legitimate, desirable, and fun in creating knots for unique, attractive, finished pieces. Do remember that it is not how many knots you know, but how creatively you use them that determines the success of a piece.

Another idea of Clove Hitching is to use the back of the knot, too. Learn to reverse your tie and do the Hitch backward, or turn the work over, or inside out, tie the Hitches desired, then return to the front and continue to work from the right side.

Set up at least eight cords for practice in making the Clove Hitch patterns and chains that follow. Do work with relatively thick cords at first and, where possible, with two shades or colors. The formations also show up more vividly in nylon and a hard-finish smooth cord rather than with fuzzy textured jutes and soft cotton twines.

Single diagonal bars in one direction are alternated with triple short diagonal bars in the opposite direction. Anchor cords are picked up and used where needed, then reworked into the horizontal bars. When end cords will be used as anchor cords throughout, make these two cords much longer than the central cords to avoid adding cords constantly. From a belt by Sarajane Bitterman.

Diagonal bars are used in differing lengths within an area created by longer bars. In working with Clove Hitches exclusively it is not so important to have multiples of four cords. Any number of cords may be used in bars that can start and stop anywhere the designer decides. They may be angled singly and in groups, they may meet or not meet. Feel free to design your own directions and multiples for Clove Hitching. Detail by Joan Michaels Paque.

Photo, Henry Paque

In the chain demonstrations, the finished chain is shown first so you know what you are aiming for. The knotting plan follows; and a third set of cords may be shown to illustrate possible variations. Chains only appear complicated-looking at first. Concentrate on them a few seconds and tie one or two: you'll be amazed at how really simple the procedures and principles are. Soon, you'll be intertwining cords in progressions and patterns that you work out for yourself.

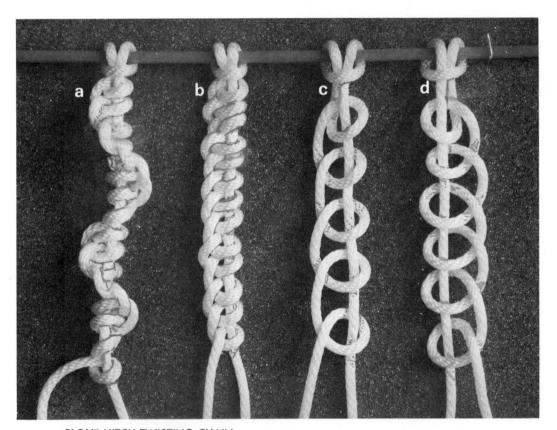

CLOVE HITCH TWISTING CHAIN

One of the easiest variations of the Clove Hitch is the chain. Using two strands, continue tying the Clove Hitch on one side only of the other strand. Begin with the first loop over the anchor cord and continue tying the loops over the anchor strand as shown. (A) The cord will twist or (B) it may be worked to lie flat. (C) Tie with the left strand over the right for the entire length or (D) the right strand over the left. The knotting strand will be used up more rapidly than the anchor, so figure and mount lengths unevenly when making these chains. For bulky effects knot the Clove Hitches over several anchor cords.

ALTERNATING HALF HITCH CHAIN

For an Alternating Half Hitch chain simply
tie one loop (a Half Hitch) of the left strand
over the right strand. Alternate and tie one
loop of the right strand over the left strand.
Repeat, always alternating the strand. These
may be tied close together or far apart for
different effects. They may also be tied with
multiples of two or more strands as shown.
This chain can be used for curves and verticals, for interiors and endings. It may be
used within Square Knots, combined for a
rougher motif with unknotted floating cords.
*Remember, when knotting chains, begin the
first loop over the anchor cord rather than
under it as with horizontal hitching.*

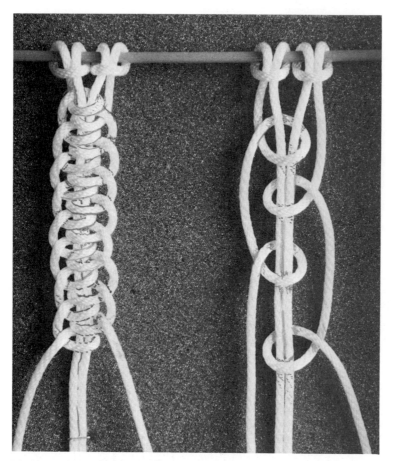

SINGLE ALTERNATING CLOVE HITCH CHAIN

The principle of creating all chains is alternating the two loops of the Hitch over anchor cords in varying progressions. The chain *(left)* is made with four cords. Each outside cord is alternately knotted over the two central anchor cords. Read the demonstration at right: observe that one Half Hitch is made with the left strand over the two anchor cords, then one Half Hitch with the right strand. Then the second half of each Hitch is performed also alternating the left and right strands.

When making chains, outer knotting cords always deplete more rapidly than the anchor cords. To knot a belt, for example, fold cords unevenly before mounting so the outer strands are two and a half to three times as long as the anchor strands.

Detail *(right)*. The same chain with seven cords; two on the left are alternated with two on the right over three anchor cords.

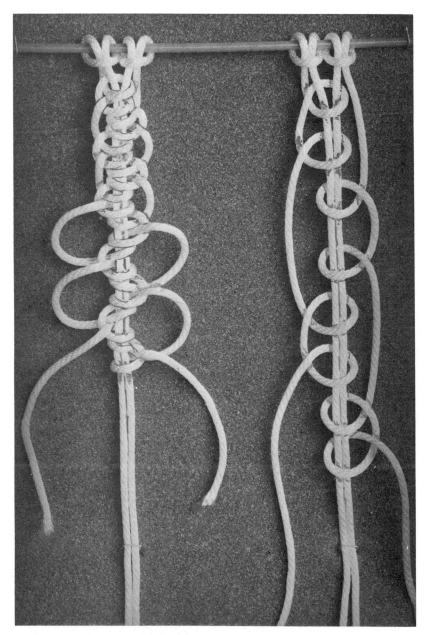

ALTERNATING CLOVE HITCH CHAIN

For this chain, tie both loops of the Clove Hitch over the anchor cord first with the left strand, then with the right strand. For a variation, accentuate the curve that results between the knots for another design motif. Try putting beads on these curves for another surface treatment.

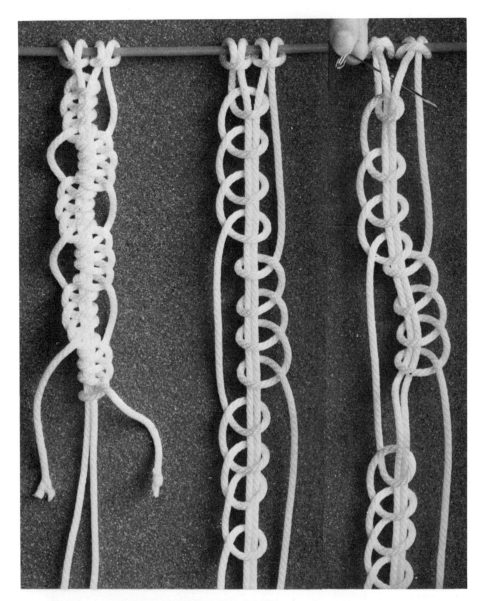

DOUBLE ALTERNATING CLOVE HITCH CHAIN

Now try two Clove Hitches, or four loops, tying with each outside strand
for another alternating chain. These strands were all the same length;
note how quickly the knotting cords are used.

And when ripping out or undoing these chains, simply lift the anchor
cords from the top and pull through rather than untie the knots.

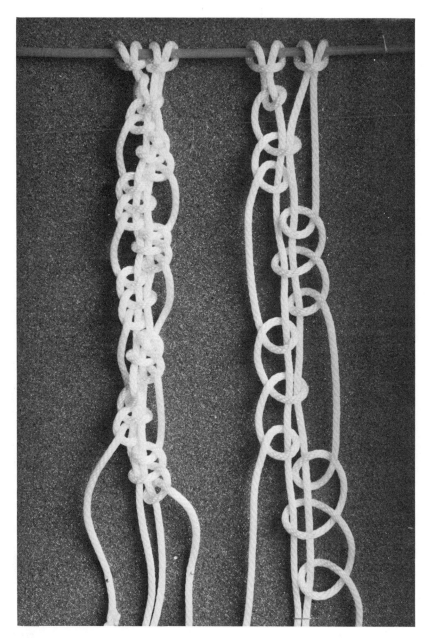

VARIED ALTERNATIVES

For still another chain, alternate the Hitches over different numbers of anchor cords. Here, the first and third Hitch are made over one anchor; the second Hitch over two anchors. It is repeated from both sides. Try your own variations.

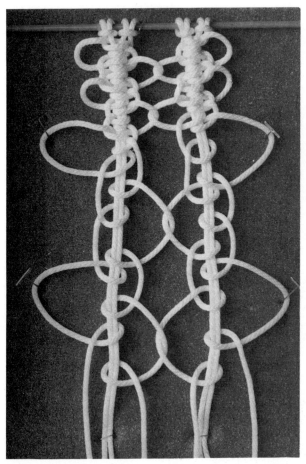

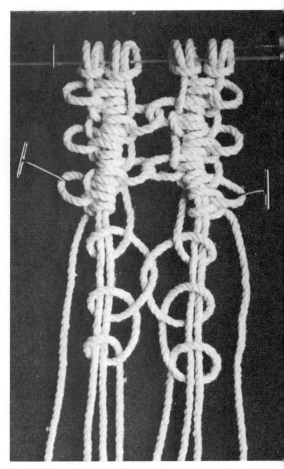

INTERTWINING CHAINS

Now try intertwining some of the chains. Using two sets of
four cords, accentuate the curves of the knotting cords
holding them with a pin when tying. Intertwine these curves
from one set of cords with the other, as shown. You can do
this with any multiple of cords. You can make them tight
or loose. You can make them with scores of cords as wide
as you like. Use them in wall hangings, for jewelry, belts,
purses, vests.

Intertwined single alternating Clove Hitches in nylon braid
(left). Intertwined alternating double Clove Hitches in cotton
seine twine *(right)*.

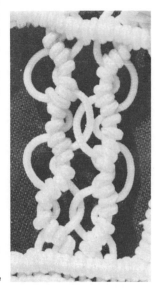

Detail *(right)*. Joan Michaels Paque. Alternating Hitches with
every other two loops intertwined.

Photo, Henry Paque

LARK'S HEAD CHAINS

Vertical chain Clove Hitching can become confusing without your realizing what is happening. By purposely or accidentally reversing the direction and tying order of one of the loops, another appearance results in the knot. If you reverse a cord accidentally, and like the resulting knot, you often wonder how it happened and strive to do it again. So it is easier to learn what happens when you loop the Hitches differently and then you can utilize these differences to advantage—and on purpose.

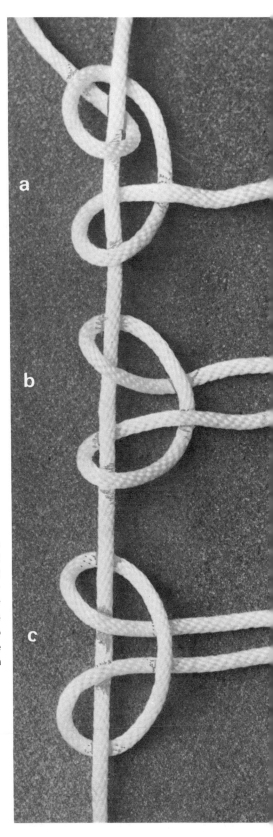

a. The vertical Clove Hitch is tied with the first loop originating from *under* the anchor cord, and the second loop is brought *over* the anchor cord. The knotting cord then emerges over the curve and between the loops.

b. For the vertical chains shown, your first loop is *reversed* and begins over the anchor cord followed by second loop over the anchor cord; the knotting cord again emerges over and between the loops.

c. A third variation is to tie the first loop over the cord as in (b), but then bring the knotting cord *under* the anchor around and through to result in a Lark's Head knot—the same used for mounting. Now the knotting cord emerges under the curve and between the loops. Observe the difference in the resulting bar between the two loops. Chains tied with the Lark's Head have a different appearance from those tied with reverse Half Hitches or Clove Hitches.

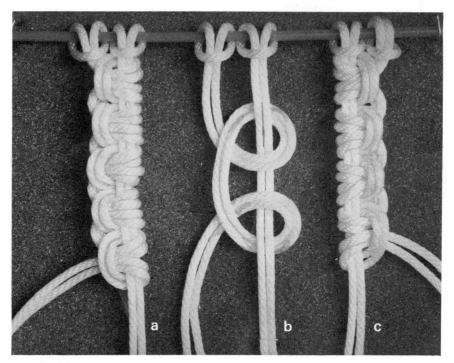

SINGLE VERTICAL LARK'S HEAD CHAIN

The Lark's Head chain may be tied with two cords or four as illustrated. It doesn't matter which cords are used for knotting, the right or left.

a. Illustrates knotting the left cords over the anchor to result in a ridge on the left side. (C) has a right side ridge resulting from knotting the right cords over the anchor cords.

b. To make the vertical Lark's Head, bring the cord over the anchor, make the loop around to the top, and bring the cord through. For the second loop, begin with the cord *under* the anchor, loop it around over the anchor and through the curve. Correctly tied, the knot will have a ridge over the two loops.

Right, detail knotted with cords divided into three and three. For the left chain, the first left cord is knotted over two anchors. For the right chain the farthest right cord is knotted over two anchors. They are held in the middle by one knot tied over four anchors *and* the right tying cord. Note the woven motif also using six cords. Detail, Joan Michaels Paque.

Photo, Henry Paque

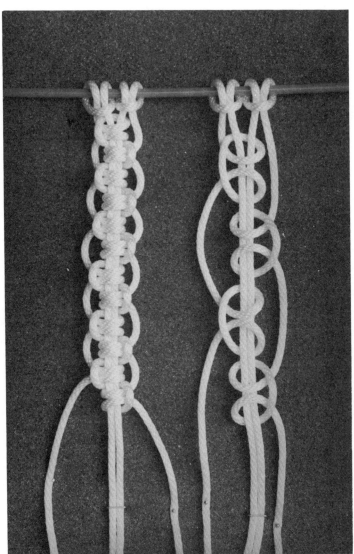

ALTERNATING LARK'S HEAD CHAIN

Alternating Lark's Head chain using four cords: both loops of one complete Lark's Head are made on each side of the anchor cord in alternating order with the left and right knotting cords. To rip any of the chains, simply lift out the anchor cords from the top.

The same alternating Lark's Head tied closely together using six cords: two cords each for knotting from each side over two anchor cords. The curve with the negative area next to the chain results automatically when each subsequent knot is made. It may be accentuated, if desired, by pulling it out and allowing it to protrude more before the first loop of each subsequent knot is tied.

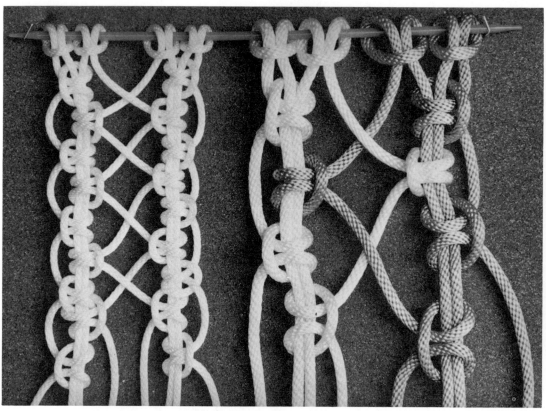

ALTERNATING LARK'S HEAD INTERTWINE

Look complicated? It isn't. And it's fun. It's hard to follow in the one-color lightweight nylon braid *(left)* so the progression is shown in two colors *(right)*. Using eight cords, two groups of four share anchor cords at different points. Only the fourth and fifth cords vary and cross over. A word description would take paragraphs; but the photo is easy to follow in the heavier two-color cord. Once mastered, it's a great knotting device for Macramé, and also to keep children intrigued for hours. Try these with more sets of cords, with varying hues of one color and with contrasting colors to see the many effects possible.

More variations of the alternating Lark's Head chains by Joan Michaels Paque. ❯ All are easy to follow after you've done one or two of those shown on the previous pages.

Photo, Henry Paque

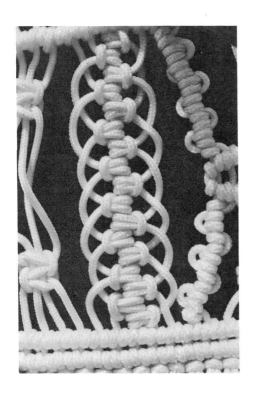

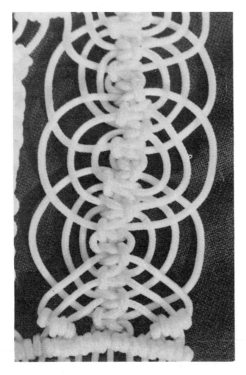

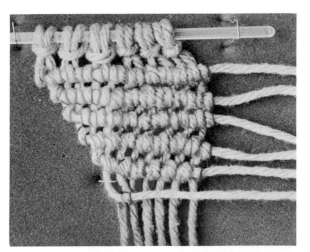

SOLID ANGLED CLOVE HITCH

The Clove Hitch, worked in groups of horizontal and vertical rows, can result in an interesting angled motif. Because the direction change is so pronounced it is attractive for monotone cords as well as with colors.

For a sampler, begin mounting at least six cords (twelve strands) of a soft cord. We used three mountings each of two colors of knitting worsted for the demonstration.

1. For each horizontal row pick up a new anchor cord from the left and Clove Hitch each vertical cord in turn over the horizontal anchors. Extend each anchor cord to the right. Knot six bars and the work will angle toward the right as shown.

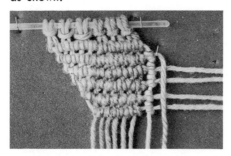

2. Use the first top horizontal anchor cord and place cords vertically. Knot vertical Clove Hitches using the other cords that extend to the right. Or turn the work sideways and the procedure will be the same as tying horizontal Clove Hitches. Each cord now becomes an anchor for a row of vertical Hitches.

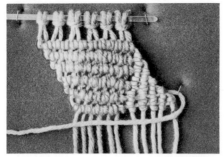

3. When these are all used up, reverse the directions of the anchor and create another series of horizontal bars that will angle toward the left.

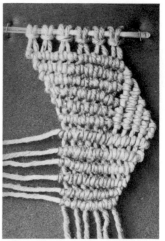

4. Finished rows of horizontal bars right to left.

5. Using those cords for a series of vertical Clove Hitches will result in another direction change.

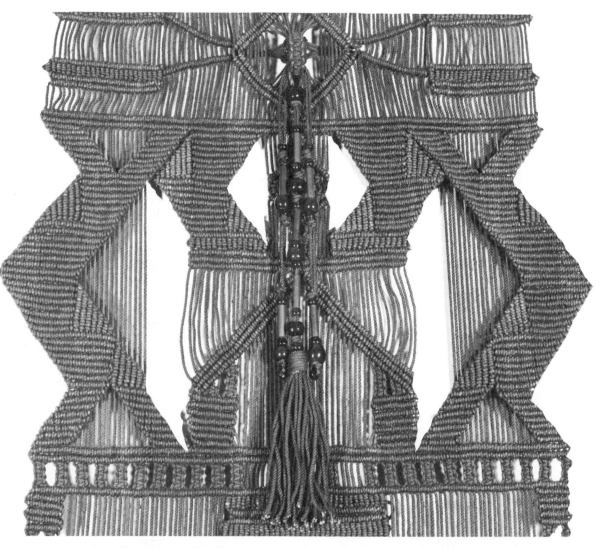

DARK RED AND BLUE CORD with PAKISTAN BEADS *(detail)*. Gerald P. Hodge.
Cotton Chalk Line dyed. The angled Clove Hitch is used with horizontals and
verticals, with negative spaces and floating cords in this beautifully composed
detail from a six-foot-long hanging.

Courtesy, artist

VEST. Nancy Larson. Solid angling of
the Clove Hitch used with circular move-
ments and all other directions of Clove
Hitching in this carefully color-controlled
vest.

Courtesy, artist

HANGING. Joan Michaels Paque. 36"
high. Some angling used along with
Lark's Head chains. Central chains stand
out alone, but inside and outside borders are Lark's Head chains intertwined
with alternating Square Knots. Some
loose and tight weaving also. Square
Knots and wrapping.

Photographed at Art Independent,
Lake Geneva, Wisconsin

SWALLOWS NEST. Doris Hoover. 18" x 24". Wools, silks, cottons, and beads worked from a weathered chair leg. Macramé, braiding, and detached button-hole knots.   *Photo, Margaret Vaile*

MACRAMÉ ON EXHIBITION at the Richard Feigen Gallery, Chicago. Claire Zeisler. Freestanding and wall-hung sculptural Macramé.   *Photo, Jonas Dovydenas*

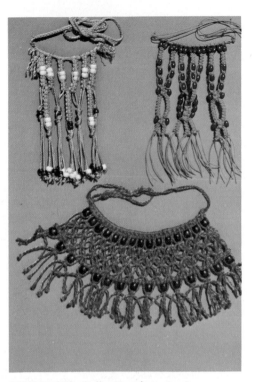

HIM. Louise Todd. Knotted animal worked over a core of clothesline. *Courtesy, artist*

NECKLACES. Sally Davidson (top), Lynn Needham (bottom), Yarn, carpet thread, and beads. *Photo, author*

FLOOR PIECE. Babs Burchall. Plastic strips square knotted. *Photo, author*

NECKLACES. Helen Hennessey. Combinations of varied knitting yarns, some with Swistraw and ceramic beads. *Photo, author*

ANGLED MACRAMÉ. Mary Baughn. 5' x 2½'. White, gold and pink yarn combining the angled motif with alternating Square Knots and chains. Square Knot buttons add surface dimension.

Detail from left. Mary Baughn. Angles have negative areas through which a Square Knot chain is worked.

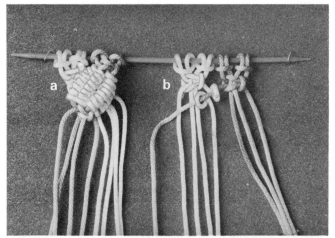

THE BERRY KNOT

One can achieve another dimension for a Macramé surface by knotting a berry, a variation using Clove Hitches. The finished Berry Knot (a) is begun by (b) mounting four cords (eight strands) of one or two colors. Make a Square Knot at the top of each set of four strands. Use each strand of the right group in turn for an anchor cord held diagonally and Clove Hitched with the strands in the left group.

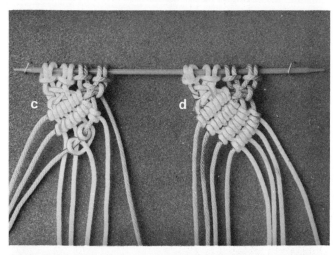

(c) Three strands from the right group have been Clove Hitched in diagonal bars with strands from the left group. (d) When all strands are tied, the anchor cords will not show. In this way colors can be brought through the work in different places, sometimes disappearing and reappearing.

(e) Now taking the four anchor cords, prepare to make a Square Knot. As you pull the outer knotting cords, place your finger behind the work and push up until the form is rounded. Tie a Square Knot.
(f) With the remaining four cords at the right side tie another Square Knot to hold the berry in shape.

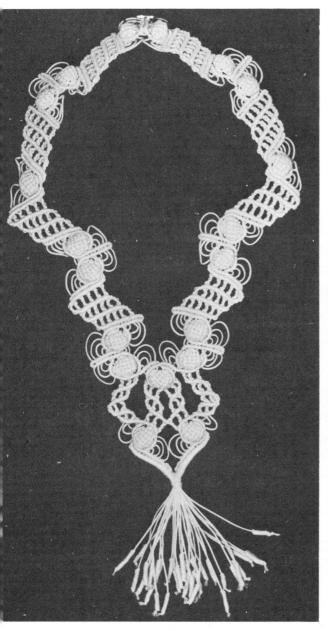

BERRY NECKLACE. Joan Michaels Paque. Thin polypropylyne braided white cord. The Berry Knots are worked into a frame of Clove Hitches. Here the reverse side of the Clove Hitch is used. The work is turned over to make the Clove Hitches, then the rows are poked to the front to raise them.

Collection, Dona Meilach

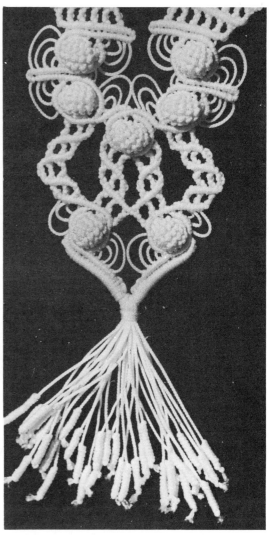

Detail of Berry Knots (*above*).

7

Increasing
Your Knot Vocabulary

As you become proficient with basic knots, you may wish to broaden your knowledge of knots for variety and interest. Additional knots that adapt most successfully to Macramé are illustrated: the Overhand Knot, Chinese Crown, Josephine, Coil, and Monkey's Fist. More ideas for working cords are shown, too, including weaving, making tassels, and fringing.

It is not necessary to limit yourself to these knots because they are shown in a Macramé book. Knots used in crochet, embroidery, lace-making, and tatting may all be incorporated. A few teachers teach braiding with multiple cords, such as a pillow lace technique shown in the de Dillmont encyclopedia. It is not demonstrated here because none of the more than a thousand examples submitted for the book illustrated this braid in a finished piece.

Joan Paque shares variations of basic knots she often uses. For additional knot sources refer to the Bibliography and specifically to needlework and knotting encyclopedias. Select knots that are personally appealing for your own designs.

To learn the new knots, mount a minimum of eight cords (sixteen strands) on a holder and practice the procedures first, to learn them: second, to develop your own combinations. Use two or three cords, intertwine knots, and combine them with the basic knots for infinite design possibilities.

Names of knots vary from source to source, but you'll soon recognize knots and be able to follow visual illustrations more quickly than written instructions. It is not necessary to learn complex knots because so many attractive effects can be achieved with simple knots. The Overhand Knot best illustrates this point.

The Overhand Knot is one of the simplest and most versatile auxiliary knots used in Macramé. You used it to tie your holding line around a pin. Simply make a loop and bring one end around the cord through the loop and pull. Use the Overhand Knot for endings, to hold beads in place, and for design within a work.

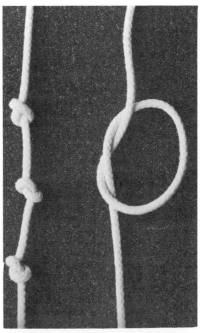

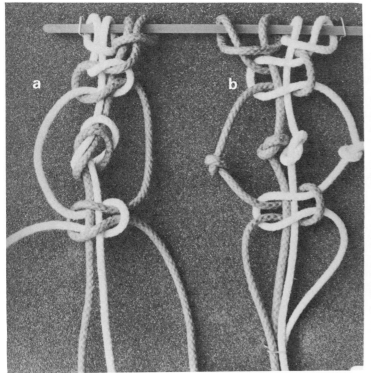

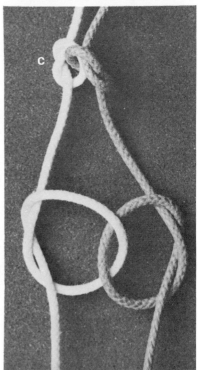

a. The Overhand Knot tied with the anchor cords amid Square Knots; and,

b. Made on individual anchor cords between a Square Knot and on each knotting cord.

c. Overhand Knots intertwined using one cord for each knot. It may be tied with four cords also.

The Overhand Knot tied with alternate strands and with multiple strands in varying progressions and lengths is simple to work: the results belie the simplicity. For alternate Overhand Knotting, tie an Overhand Knot with each pair of cords for the first row. For the second row, drop the first cord and tie each of the next pairs of cords. For subsequent rows, repeat rows one and two. Knots may be far apart or close together with a diamond area resulting between.

The same progression of alternating knots as above has another appearance when tied tightly and close together.

Pairs of cords are intertwined and then knotted in the same alternate knotting progression as above.

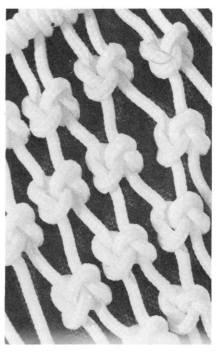

Overhand Knots are used to hold beads in place and also as knots alone for design. Overhand Knots also make excellent motifs for endings and to prevent fraying ends from unraveling.

Overhand Knots intertwined using four strands; two together for each knot.

Detail photos, Henry Paque

Two Overhand Knots tied next to each other vertically.

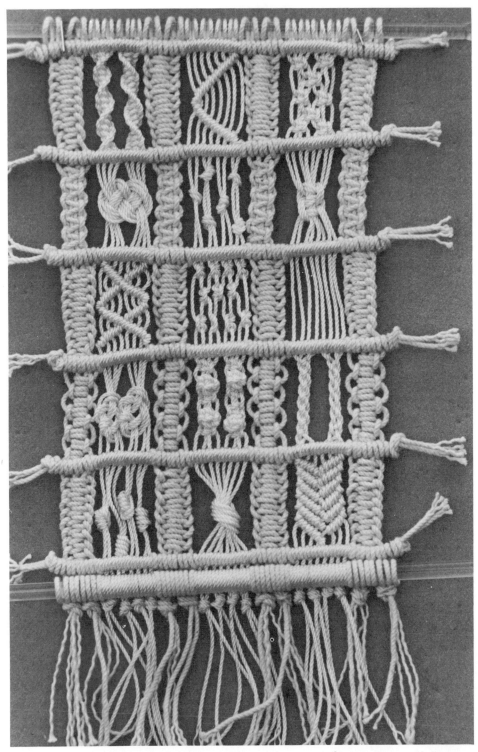

KNOT SAMPLER. Sally Davidson. Cotton and nylon seine twine, 14″ high, 10″ wide. Sally Davidson mounts nylon and cotton twine and ties each knot or variation in a rectangle by itself to learn how different knots look in different cords. Drawing (*right*) is used as reference and also as an identifying chart of knots used.

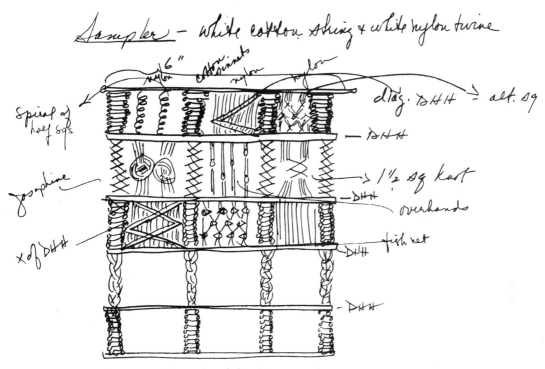

Drawing of sampler *(left)*. Sally Davidson. Drawings are made on a graph
paper so they may be blown up in a
proportionate size for a large hanging.

SAILOR'S SAMPLER OF KNOTS. 48"
high, 30" wide. A variety of braids becomes the frame for samples of knots
placed in a pattern and mounted on a
wooden board. Nineteenth century.

*Courtesy, The Mariners Museum,
Newport News, Va.*

THE JOSEPHINE KNOT

The Josephine Knot, also referred to as the "Garrick Bend," is a decorative knot used within a pattern or by itself for a belt or jewelry. It may be tied with two, four, or any multiple of cords and knots intertwined. As with many knots, the diagrams make the procedure look more complex than it is. Carefully following the directions will result in a beautiful, easy-to-do knot. It may be tied loosely or tightly. If loosely tied cords tend to slip, a dab of glue at the back will hold them. Two cords (or four strands) are used in the demonstration.

a. Make a loop, as shown, with the left cords.

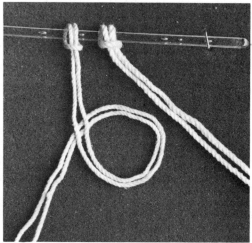

b. Bring the right cords over the left loop and under the loose left strands.

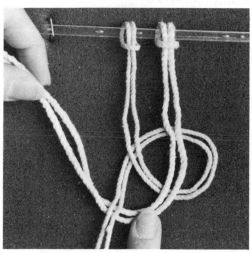

c. Bring right cords around and over top left, *under* next pair of cords, over the right cord and under the original loop in the same way you would weave a cord; over, under, over and under.

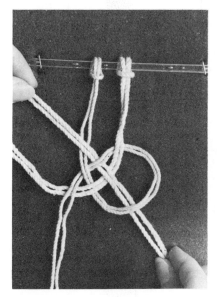

d. Pull to even and begin loop for next knot. Repeat.

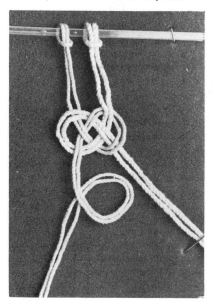

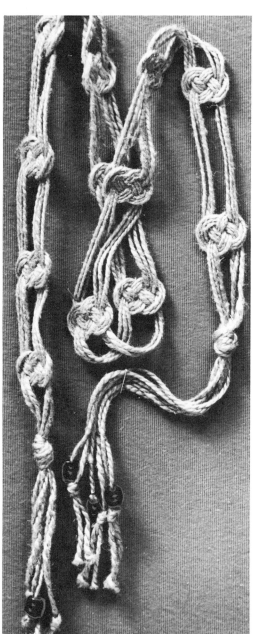

A belt of Josephine Knots. Lynn Needham. Jute. Beads and Overhand Knot endings.

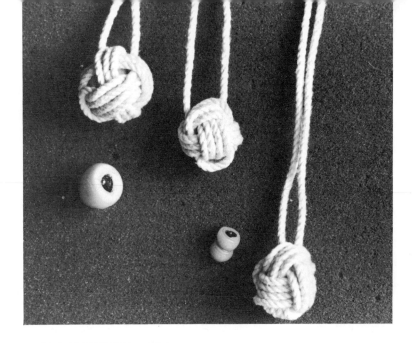

THE MONKEY'S FIST

The Monkey's Fist is a three-dimensional knot tied over a bead or other hard object to give it form and solidity. It is usually employed as a hanging motif from ends, from horizontal rods or for belt, jewelry, and purse endings. It can be sewn to a purse or vest and used as a button. The knot may be created from cords that remain after knotting. It may be added to the work wherever desired. Size is determined by the size of bead used in center. For larger knots, hold the fingers wider apart to allow more space for the center bead.

a. Wind cord vertically around fingers several times, making last wind at right over one finger.

b. Bring cord behind windings and around to front.

c. Continue to wind horizontally several times, bringing the last wind through top loops.

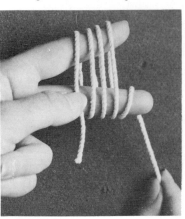

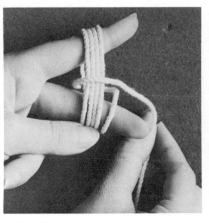

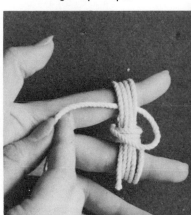

d. Remove fingers and insert ½″ diameter or larger bead in center.

e. Bring end of cord through bottom loops.

f. Tighten each circuit of cord consecutively into place.

g. Turn knot around as you work and continue to tighten each cord until a firm covering for the bead results.

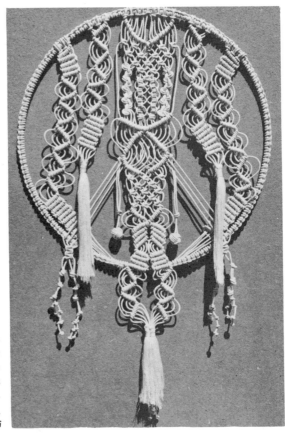

TONDO WITH TASSELS. Berni Gorski. ⅛″ cotton traverse cord. 24″ diameter, 37″ long. Monkey's Fists added as a balancing motif for the fringes.
Photo, Henry Gorski

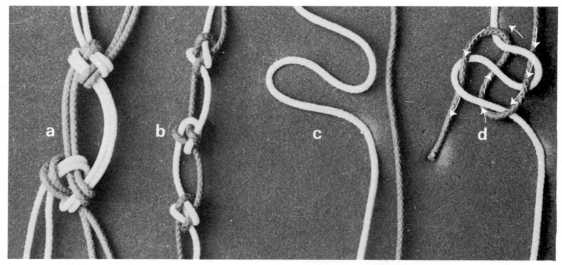

CHINESE CROWN KNOT

The Chinese Crown Knot has the appearance of a soft pillow when knotted of thick braided cords with two, four, or more strands. It may be used close together, far apart, or tied with alternate strands in each row.

(a) Finished knot tied with four cords and (b) with two cords. (c) Place the left cord on the board with two opposing bends as shown. Wind the right cord through the bends of the left cord from top in direction of arrows (d). It goes under the top cord then over the next two. Bend it and go back under all three. Bend again and bring it down over two cords, under one, and tighten.

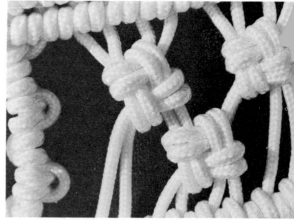

The same knot has a different appearance when four strands are tied.

Detail photos, Henry Paque

Chinese Crown Knot in two strands using alternate strands for each row.

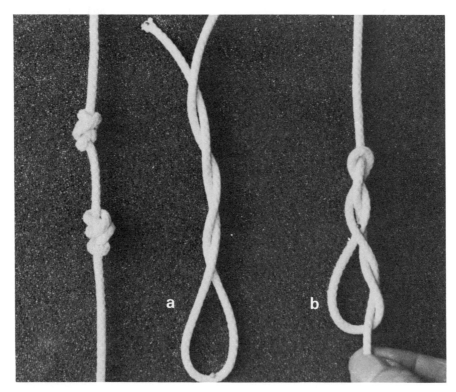

COIL KNOT

The Coil Knot is a version of the Hangman's Knot. It may be used in the middle of work or at ends. (a) Fold a cord back on itself so it makes a loop. Twist the loose end over the longer cord several times. (b) Bring loose end down from behind and through to front of loop and pull gently until the winds form a coil.

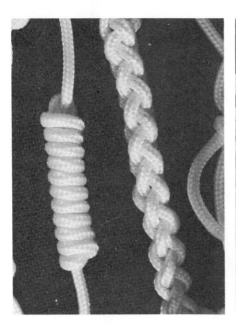

The coil may be created of many winds onto itself.

Detail photos, Henry Paque

It may be wound around another cord by encompassing the second cord as the first is wound.

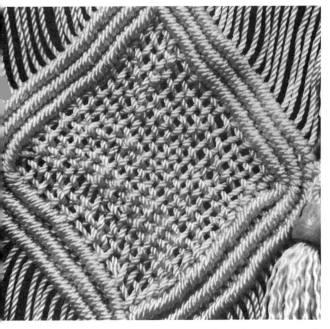

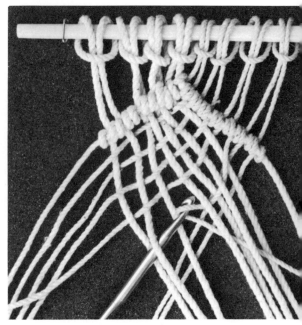

In addition to knotting, there are various decorative effects that may be used. Here, cords are woven within a Clove Hitch diamond.

Weaving several cords is easier if you work them over and under one another with a crochet hook.

Use weaving to create a simple, light relief among heavy knotted chains.

Or the cords may be placed so all in one direction are behind those in the opposite direction.

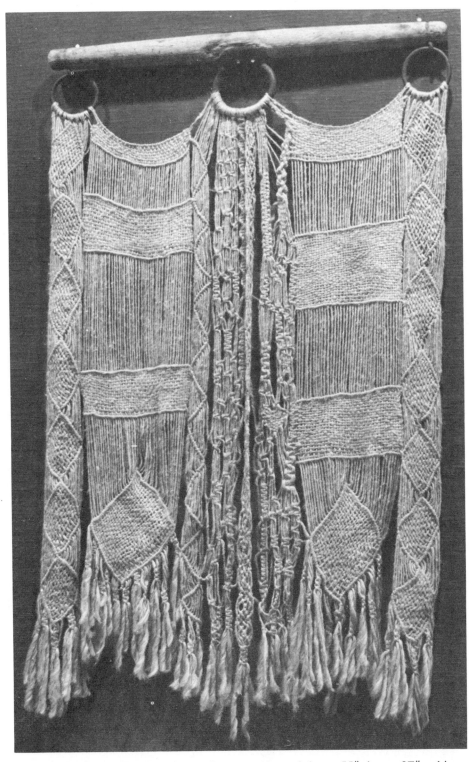

SINGLETREE HANGING. Clara Creager. Natural jute, 55″ long, 37″ wide. Mounted on a singletree used for harnessing horses, the piece is composed of Square Knots and Half Hitches, woven rectangles and diamond shapes, and areas of floating cords.

Collection, Mr. MacDonald, Virgin Islands
Photo, Arthur Burt, Inc.

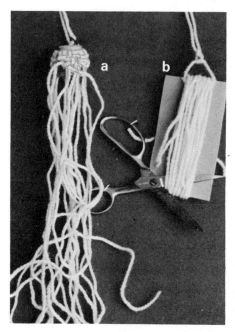

TASSELS

Many of the hangings and accessories have tassels and fringes, important adjuncts to Macramé. Both may be done with knotting.

Tassels may be made by wrapping the cord over a piece of cardboard and winding another cord near the top to hold the pieces together. But a tassel may be created with Square Knots as shown.

a. Mount eight cords of yarn or string on a holding line. Tie the holding line around an object such as a spool from thread. Then make three rows of alternating Square Knots.
b. Wind cord (knitting yarn is used here) around a piece of cardboard cut to length of desired tassel. Tie a cord through the loops at the top. Cut the loops at the bottom.

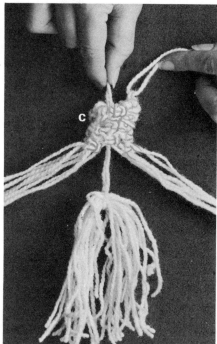

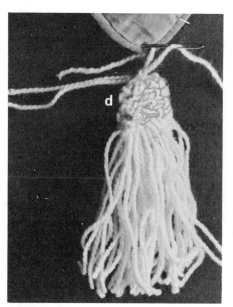

c. Remove the knotted piece from the spool. Pull the wrapped piece up through the hole of the knotted piece; pull the holding line taut.

d. Tassels are sewn to the corner of a pillow with a needle. They may also be knotted directly or sewn to the end of a hanging. Extra ends from a hanging may be brought down through the tassel and become part of the ending as a finishing technique.

FRINGES

Fringes are used as an added finishing detail for hangings, hems of garments such as vests, ponchos, capes; on blankets, rugs, pillows, etc. A fringe may have all the colors of the original item, or it may contrast with the original. Sometimes, multiple colors are used in fringing, too, depending upon the colors of the piece to which it is attached.

Mount the cords the desired width apart and tie a Lark's Head. The edge of the object actually serves as a horizontal mounting line.

Often, it is easier to pull the cords through with a crochet hook. For fine fabric, each cord may have to be threaded with a needle to penetrate the material.

Once mounted, the cords may be knotted in any pattern desired and made any length.

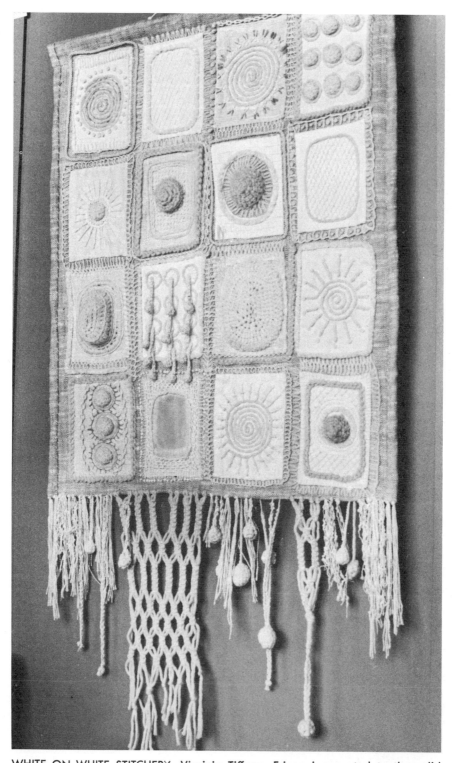

WHITE ON WHITE STITCHERY. Virginia Tiffany. Fringe is mounted to the solid fabric edge of a stitchery and worked. Several kinds of knotting patterns are used, Clove Hitch chains, Monkey's Fists, and combinations of knots and braids.

Photographed at Art Independent, Lake Geneva, Wisconsin

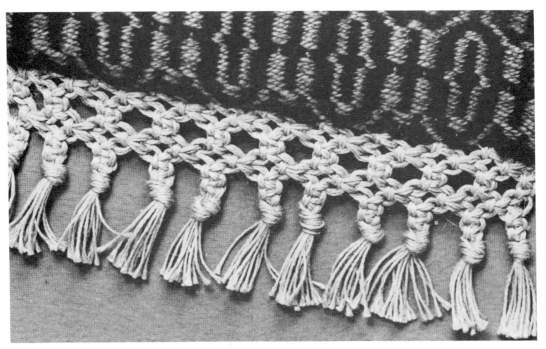

Stana Coleman has added fringe to the bottom of a fabric purse and knotted it with alternate Square Knots held by bundled Overhand Knots.

Fringe added to arm opening of a corduroy cape by Lynn Needham. The yarn was stitched through the fabric; no Lark's Head used. The first row is a straight horizontal Clove Hitch. Second and third rows are spaced and Clove Hitched in a scalloped design.

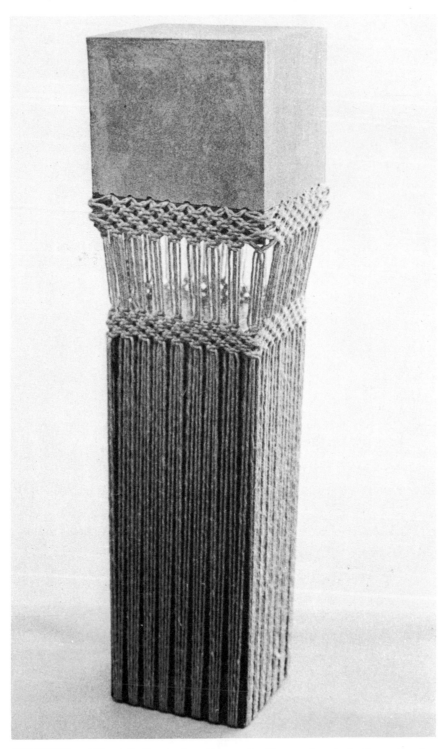

SCULPTURE. Mikael C. Carstenjen. Macramé with wood and plastic rectangles, 40" high, 12" square. The transparent portion is clear plastic, the top is a brightly painted wood cube.

Macramé
and Mixed Materials

8

Mixing cords with various art media and knotting with other art techniques are fascinating aspects of contemporary art. This illustrates the trend away from tradition and presents innovations already developed by creative artists who dare to be uninhibited in the use of materials and combinations.

Macramé is being successfully combined with ceramics and appears both as an integral part of the design or as an adjunct for hanging ceramic pots and sculptures. Mikael Carstanjen utilizes Macramé with hand-blown glass, wood, and plastic cubes. Because of the see-through quality of knotting, it weds miraculously with clear materials for three-dimensional forms that often have the illusion of hanging precariously in space.

Combining Macramé with other textiles as an expressive statement seems absolutely natural; yet only a few artists have adapted the knotting as a major portion of the work as opposed to a finishing fringe. Lorraine Ohlson and Libby Platus both have worked Macramé in a sensitive, creative manner, integrating it with stitchery and rug-making methods. Many weavers use Macramé, and there is a trend toward more creative combinations of the two techniques. Nonloom and cardboard weaving are natural companions to the nontool knotting.

The pieces shown are offered to stimulate you to think in terms of the kinds of unrelated things that can be imaginatively related when the artist has every possible technique at his command.

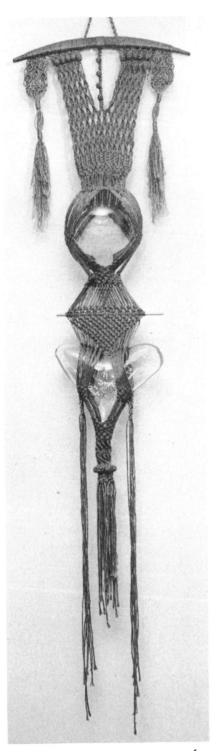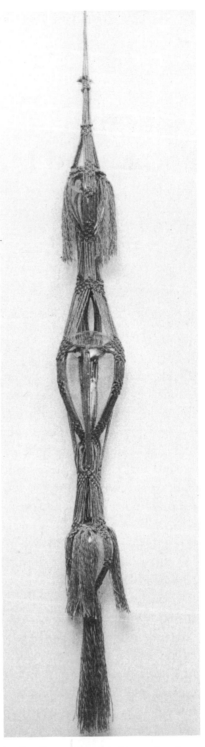

BLOWN GLASS WITH MACRAMÉ. Mikael C. Carstanjen. Jute and glass. Macramé beautifully designed to hold clear, hand-blown glass shapes which add three-dimensional areas to the otherwise flat knotting. The piece at left was begun from below the large glass ball beginning with a circle of cords, then worked in both directions. The piece at right was begun from the top and cords added as needed.

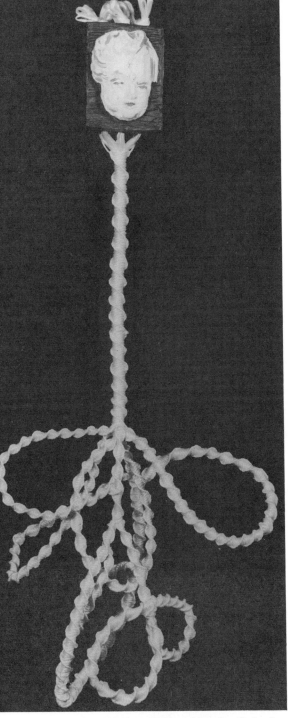

ACRYLIC ANGEL. Shirley Marein. Polyethe-
lyne sennit of twisted Half Hitches with a
ceramic head mounted on wood.

Photo, Juan Valdivia Aranda

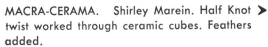

MACRA-CERAMA. Shirley Marein. Half Knot ➤
twist worked through ceramic cubes. Feathers
added.

Photo, Juan Valdivia Aranda

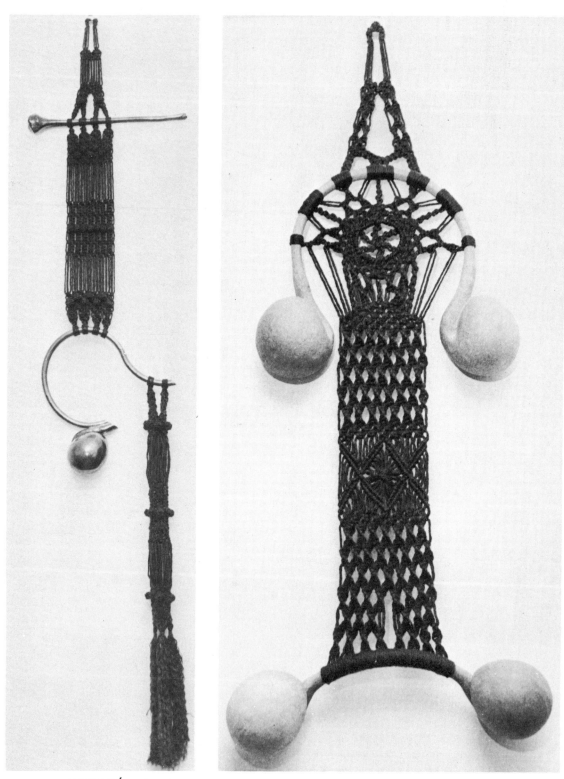

MACRAMÉ WITH CERAMICS.   Mikael C. Carstenjen. Approximately 6' high.
Black-dyed jute with handmade ceramic forms.

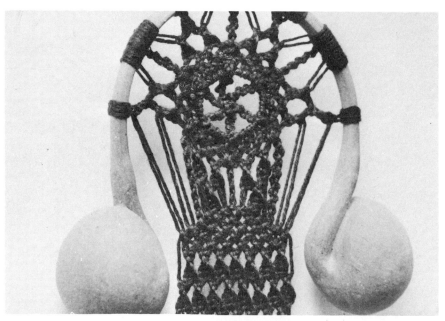

Detail showing the beginning of piece from a center circle.

Working board devised by Mr. Carstenjen for working Macramé with three-dimensional shapes so the shapes can hang freely and the knotting worked so it will hang straight. A guillotine-like stand is created. The board at bottom can crank up and down to work the knots at convenient heights. Board and frame were marked off into one-inch squares.

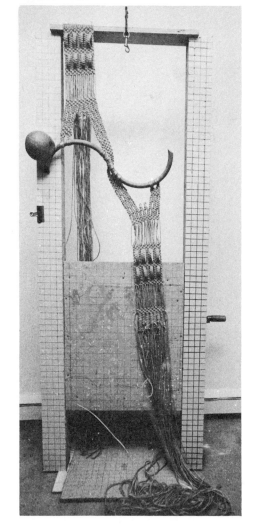

BLUE AND PURPLE. Michi Ouchi. Woven top is beautifully combined with Macramé at the bottom with open and tight areas of Clove Hitching and wrapping. Braiding added.

Courtesy, artist

SUN HANGING.   Esther S. Dendel. Wool and weaving warp, 48″ high, 26″ wide. Background is Clove Hitched and some trim is Half Knotted. Sun and rays are woven on cardboard, then stitched to background.

RUG HOOKING WITH MACRAMÉ.   Lorraine Ohlson, 36″ high, 48″ wide. Hooking done in areas on linen backing, then trimmed. Knotting cords attached at inner curves and worked toward edges using same yarn used for hooking.

MIXED MEDIA HANGING.   Libby Platus. Seine twine mounted on driftwood ➤ with holes drilled. Leather, lambswool pelts, wool, reindeer yarn, 10′ high, 7′ wide. Combines knotting, collage, and stitchery techniques.

9

Fashions and Accessories

The same ingenuity and imagination that craftsmen are applying to wall hangings and sculptural Macramé are appearing in fashions made by knotting. Macramé clothes boast marvelous fringes and incorporate beading that give the fabrics a unique perpetually fashionable quality.

Dresses, vests, ponchos, and similar garments may be knotted in several ways. Some are designed as front and back panels which are then knotted together as a seam. A garment may be worked from one edge, the back bottom for instance, up to the top and around and down the front by adding and subtracting cords as in knitting. They may also be started from the neck and worked outward or from the shoulders and down.

There really is no precedent for designing and planning. The best solution is to use a pattern sketched on a board to the size desired. Pin cords to the pattern and work the piece as shown in the poncho on page 187. Many garments are not made even in this formal a manner; the mechanics for each garment must be individually determined and developed.

Purses and belts are always popular and, once you have made a hanging or a piece of jewelry, evolving the pattern for any utilitarian item is not too hard. Some items such as purses and belts may require a more decorative mounting than a holding bar, so the use of Picots is illustrated in this chapter. Picots are applicable to any other Macramé mounting and should be part of your total knotting knowledge.

PONCHO. Edward Sherbeyn. Jute, red wool, ceramic beads. Square Knotting, Clove Hitching, and some wrapping.

Courtesy, Edward Sherbeyn Gallery, Chicago
Photo, Christa; for Ebony

SUEDE VEST with Macramé trim. Joy
Lobell. Macramé worked from neckline
before binding. Tiny wood beads added.

PLASTIC VEST.   Mary Baughn. Strips of
plastic in alternate Square Knot pattern.
Pompoms added by knotting strips into
negative spaces between knots in front
of vest.

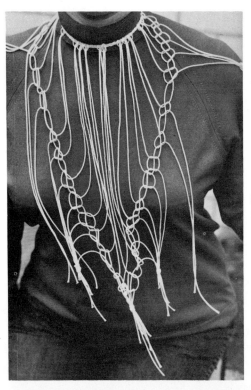

BODY JEWELRY. Susan Meilach. Nylon braid in loosely tied Square Knots.

OVERSKIRT. Dorris Akers. Waistband of Square Knots interlaced. Vertical knotting cords added to waistband bottom.

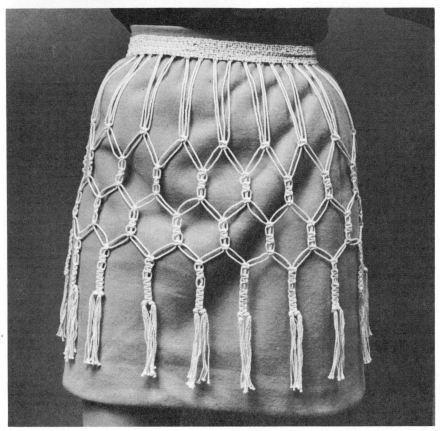

BODY COVERING. Marla
Strecher. White cotton twine. Two
views.

Courtesy, artist

PONCHO.   Dona Meilach. White Jute-Tone.

The poncho pattern was adapted from a McCall's sewing pattern. It was drawn on a Celotex board *(below left)* and a doubled holding line pinned around the neckline. Knotting cords four times the length of the pattern's depth were mounted at the neckline and used doubled. The doubled cords, completely worked in the alternate Square Knot pattern, were knotted closer together at the shoulders and farther apart at the widest portions of the pattern *(right, below)*. Final knots are pulled tight to hold. Ends are simply trimmed and left free for fringe. Any shape for clothes, jewelry, curtains, etc., may be worked in this manner— by drawing a pattern and then shaping the knotting to fit it. Manufactured clothing patterns may be adapted for vests, shirts, ponchos, and so on.

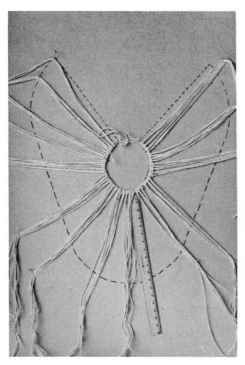

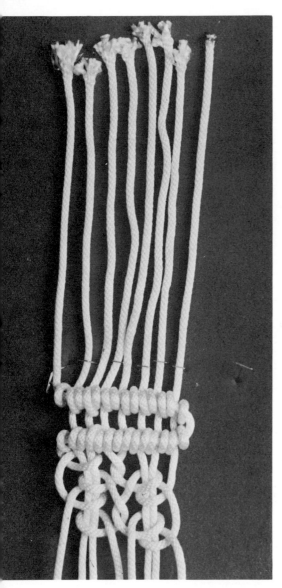

MORE METHODS FOR BEGINNING

Mounting knotting cords to a horizontal holding line will not serve every purpose for beginning specific pieces of Macramé. A fringed belt. for example, will begin directly with Clove Hitches or Square Knots several inches from the ends of the cords. So long as the cords are pinned to a board or hung so they may be tied, it is not necessary to mount with Lark's Head Knots. Neither is it always necessary to begin from an end. By Clove Hitching in the middle of a cord you can work in two directions,

Allow desired length for a belt fringe, then pin cords to board. Use an end cord for an anchor. Make the first horizontal bar with Clove Hitches and continue to knot in patterns such as Intertwined Alternating Clove Hitch Chains.

JUTE BELT. Ray W. Sawyer. Twelve cords are knotted beginning with a Square Knot about a foot from ends to allow for loose hanging cords. Alternate Square Knot pattern used throughout.

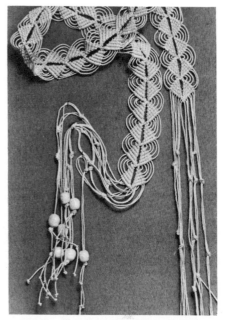

BELT.   Sarajane Bitterman. A sennit of Half Knot twists is begun from the four cords tied with an Overhand Knot.

BELT.   Sarajane Bitterman. Beginning and ending are matched. First row is the Clove Hitch in opposing diagonals. Pattern follows throughout belt.

thereby matching a pattern from the middle out: particularly desirable for belts, headbands and armbands. A belt may also be started from a ring in the center back and worked outward with or without Lark's Head mountings. It is also easier to work to a required length.

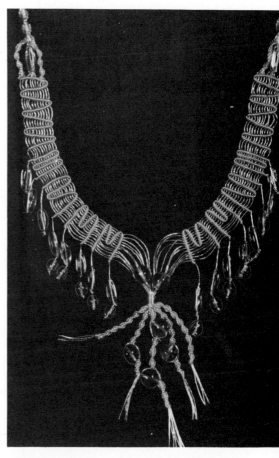

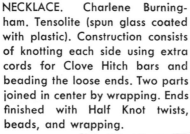

NECKLACE.   Charlene Burningham. Tensolite (spun glass coated with plastic). Construction consists of knotting each side using extra cords for Clove Hitch bars and beading the loose ends. Two parts joined in center by wrapping. Ends finished with Half Knot twists, beads, and wrapping.

Photo, Robert Burningham

DECORATIVE PICOT MOUNTINGS

Picots are small loops that form a border or edge such as is used on lace. A Picot border is often attractive for the beginning edge of a Macramé purse, hanging, dress, or vest. The principle of making a Picot is to form a loop on your knotting board over a pin, making a knot or series of knots with this loop, then Clove Hitching the strands over a horizontal line. Always allow extra length for cords that will be used for Picots.

A Picot edge is used at the top of this hanging. A dowel is sewn at the back to keep the edge taut. In soft wool, the Picots may curl up; in harder fabrics, they will stand up more.

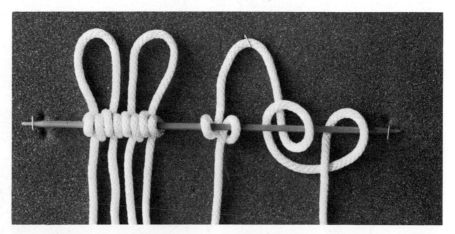

The simplest way to begin a Picot is shown finished (*at left*) and the procedure (*right*). Mount each cord to be used onto a holding line. Tie the first strand with a Clove Hitch, then pin a loop at the desired height above the holding line to knotting board and tie the second strand with a Clove Hitch. The result will be a series of loops above the holding line. This is the principle of Picots regardless of how complex the knots are in the loop above the line. Feel free to evolve your own knots for Picot decorations. Those that follow are suggestions.

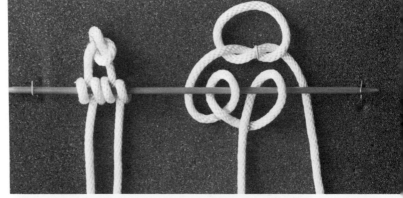

A more decorative Picot can be made by tying an Overhand Knot in the loop before Clove Hitching the second strand.

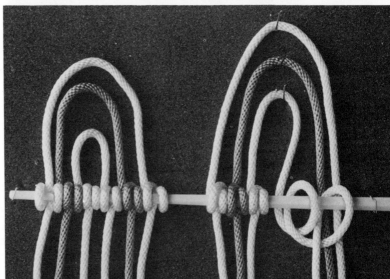

A series of loops in varying sizes makes an attractive border. Use one or more cords. Pin the three loops to the board as shown. Place a holding line over the strands and Clove Hitch them.

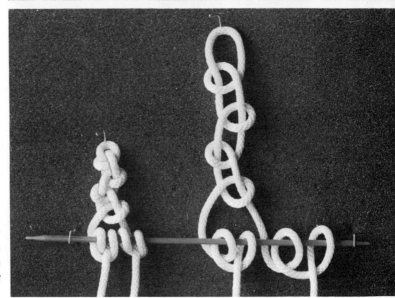

For a taller Picot that will curl and form a soft, knobby edge in a soft fiber, make the alternating Clove Hitch with two strands, then knot them to the holding line.

Six cords pinned into three loops with a Square Knot holding them together form an attractive Picot. For a taller heading, tie two or three Square Knots before placing the cords on the holding line. Make the knotting cords longer than the anchor cords.

For a heavy running scallop, attach a cord with the Lark's Head (a) and work it in Clove Hitches to be placed in a semicircle above the holding line. Attach additional knotting cords (b) as needed in the holding line, then Clove Hitch the cords from the scallop and continue to use the two cords for knotting.

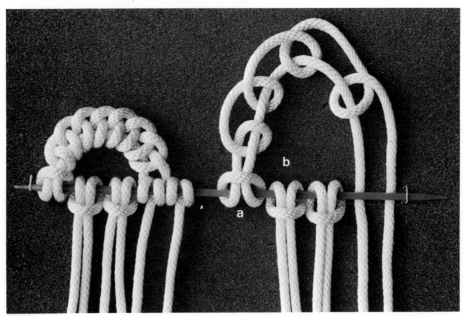

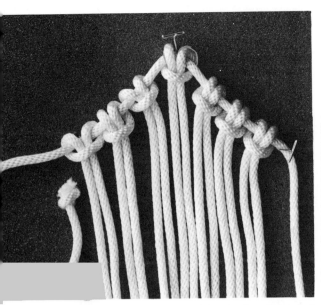

Mounting for a pointed beginning for a belt may be achieved by the angle at which the holding line is placed. Here, it is pinned to a board in a V shape upside down for the first row for a belt to be pushed through a buckle. Buckle may also become a holding line for working a belt.

Picot edges may also be made in different shapes. An Overhand Knot Picot is attached to a holding bar in the shape of a point.

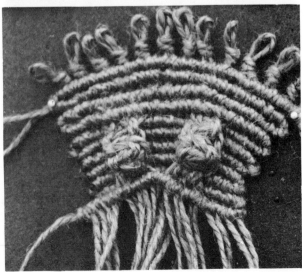

A loop extending from the Overhand Knot is actually a Picot, but used to simulate the headdress for this knotting which will resemble a mask. The holding line is pinned in a gentle curve for knotting the necessary shape. By Sally Davidson.

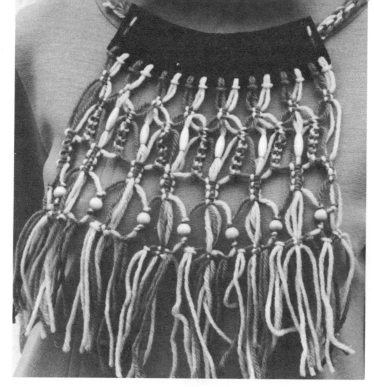

NECKPIECE. Virginia Black. Mounting may also be accomplished by making holes in a solid fabric such as suede or leather and bringing the cords through as in mounting a fringe.

NECKLACE (back view). Joan Michaels Paque. It is sometimes difficult to determine where the piece began, so adeptly can ends be made part of the pattern. "It is so easy to add cords in Clove Hitch bars," says Joan Paque, "that often I myself don't recall where a piece began." Note the Josephine Knots used to hold the piece flat at the shoulders.

PURSE. Mary Baughn. Picots give the plastic strips a gnarled decorative top edge.

BOOTS. Misty Potter. Knotting began at the bottom (instep) with Picots, then the pieces were worked up the leg with space allowed in between for lacing.
Photographed at Design West, Los Angeles

10

Macramé Furnishings

Knotted fabrics are adaptable to many uses about the home. Their decorative and functional aspects are unlimited; the only requirements are imagining where an unusual treatment is needed, then fashioning Macramé to fill that need. The following are a few ideas for using Macramé in both traditional and contemporary decorating.

Joan Michaels Paque has knotted a room-divider screen. Knotted fabrics are set into a frame and worked over horizontal wood dowels for a functional and decorative treatment. Next to it is a vase with a Macramé covering to show how subtle and beautiful Macramé can be. She also has trimmed kitchen curtains with Macramé and made curtains for entire doors and windows. All cords used are pretested for washability; some are washed before knotting to eliminate shrinkage after the piece is created to size.

Try knotting around plastic containers or flowerpots whose surfaces are worn beyond repair. Or cover any pot for an unusual decor and to tie in with a color scheme. Lampshades, bottles, temporary fireplace screens, room dividers, doorway coverings, tablecloths, doilies, hanging flower containers, valances, and scores of other items may be fashioned from knotted cords in colors and designs that are individually yours.

THREE-PANEL SCREEN AND COVERED VASE. Joan Michaels Paque.

BOTTLES COVERED WITH MACRAMÉ.
LeRoy Schwarcz. Modern interpretations
of an art begun by sailors years ago.
Photos, June Schwarcz

Spike Africa Knotting begins at the neck
of the bottle, and cords are added as
needed.

MACRAMÉ LAMPSHADE. Dorris Akers. A plain, inexpensive paper lampshade has been treated in an individual manner for conversation-piece decorating.

FLOWER HOLDER. Mary Baughn. A cornucopia shape knotted over a clear plastic cone from a milkshake container is now used to hold flowers.

CURTAIN. Peggy Wagner. Old strips of leather and wood beads have an Old World look to them used in the window of a New Mexico art gallery.

SUMMER FIREPLACE SCREEN. Dona Meilach. Colored jute adds a decorative note to fireplace opening. Holding line is a spring tension curtain rod so the piece may be converted to a window curtain.

CHAIR SEAT. Dorris Akers. A folding chair retrieved from a scrap pile was given new life by cutting away the old canvas and replacing it with knotted jute. Front and back view.

Bibliography

Anchor Manual of Needlework. 3d ed. Newton Center, Mass.: Chas. T. Branford Co.; London: Wm. Clowes and Sons Lt., 1968.

Ashley, Clifford W., *The Ashley Book of Knots.* Garden City, N.Y.: Doubleday & Co., 1944.

De Dillmont, Thérèse. *Encyclopedia of Needlework.* Mulhouse, France.

Dictionary of Macramé Knots and directions for making sixteen specific items. *Woman's Day,* 1969.

Good Housekeeping Needlecraft. New York: Hearst Corporation, 1969.

Graumont, Raoul, and Hensel, John. *Encyclopedia of Knots and Fancy Rope Work.* 4th ed. Cambridge, Maryland: Cornell Maritime Press, 1952.

Graumont, Raoul, and Wenstrom, Elmer. *Square Knot Handicraft Guide.* Cambridge, Md.: Cornell Maritime Press, 1949.

Hartung, Rolf. *Creative Textile Design.* New York: Von Nostrand-Reinhold Co., 1964.

Harvey, Virginia I. *Macramé, The Art of Creative Knotting.* New York: Van Nostrand-Reinhold Co., 1967.

Pesch, Imelda M. *Macramé Bags.* Jackson Heights, N.Y.: Pesch Art Studio, 1964.

Phillips, Mary Walker. *Step-by-Step Macramé.* New York: Golden Press, 1970.

Square Knot Booklet #1, #2 and #3. 3d ed. New York: P. C. Herwig Company, 1968.

Sources for Supplies

Twines, ropes, yarn, and other cords suitable for Macramé are available in many local stores. Logical places to look are hardware stores, building material suppliers, cordage companies, marine stores, drapery departments, wholesale and retail drapery trim suppliers, craft and hobby shops, yarn and knitting departments, weavers' suppliers, garden supply centers, etc.

Beads are stocked by local craft and hobby shops, in needlework departments, and often in toy sections. Other items such as T and U pins, plastic, wood, and brass rings for hangings, purse handles, and belt buckles often are sold at notion and sewing supply counters, handiwork and upholsterers' supply departments.

The following supply sources are listed for your convenience. They have been selected because they answered correspondence within five days to three weeks. They carry a varied selection of merchandise. No endorsement or responsibility by the author is implied.

AAA Cordage Co., Inc. 3238 N. Clark St. Chicago, Ill. 60657	Twine, rope.	Samples: $.50—twines. $.50—ropes. $1.00—twine and rope.
Carmel Valley Weavers Supply 1342 Camino Del Mar Del Mar, Cal. 92014	Wide variety imported yarns in all weights and textures. Unusual beads. Jute and sisal.	Samples: $.50.
Colonial Woolen Mills, Inc. 6501 Barberton Ave. Cleveland, O. 44102	Macramé and craft yarns.	Samples: $.50. Minimum order: $5.00.
Contessa Yarns P.O. Box 37 Lebanon, Conn. 06249	Yarns of all kinds.	Samples: $.25.

Craft Kaleidoscope 6551 Fergeson St. Broad Ripple Village Indianapolis, Md. 46220	Wide variety cords, yarns and beads. Books. Dyes.	Send stamped self- addressed envelope for supply and price lists.
Craft Yarns of Rhode Island, Inc. 603 Mineral Spring Ave. Pawtucket, R.I. 02862	All yarns for macramé. Accessories.	Samples: $.50.
Creative Handweavers P.O. Box 26480 Los Angeles, Cal. 90026	Tremendous variety of unusual yarns, cords, etc. Fleece, hair. Basketry supplies.	Wool and hair sample set: $1.00. Cotton and jute sample set: $1.00. Differs with yarns ordered. Whole- sale prices on large amounts.
Dharma Trading Co. P.O. Box 1288 Berkeley, Cal. 94701	Yarns, cordage, dyes.	Samples: $.50. Minimum order: $5.00.
Earthworks 624 W. Willow St. Chicago, Ill. 60614	Stoneware beads—10 colors. Small and large holes and sizes.	Large bead samples: $1.00.
Earthy Endeavors P.O. Box 817 Whittier, Cal. 90608	Ceramic, stoneware and porcelain glazed and unglazed beads.	Minimum order: $1.50– $3.00. Wholesale information available.
El Mercado Importing Co. 9002 8th NE Seattle, Wash. 98115	Natural Argentine and Mexican homespun sheeps- wool; natural, gray and dark brown.	Samples and price list: $.50.
Fibrec, Inc. 2815–18th Street San Francisco, Cal. 94110	Fiber reactive dyes for yarns and cords.	Free sample card of 23 dyed fabric swatches. Minimum order: $10.00. Wholesale information available.
Frederick J. Fawcett 129 South St. Boston, Mass. 02111	Linen yarns. Large variety of textures and colors.	Samples: $1.00.
Freed Co. Box 394 Albuquerque, N.M.	Coral, glass beads, wampum, Indian-made strands, turquoise. Wool fleece, mohair and wool yarns, sheepskins, goat- skins, leathers, wool carders, seashells.	Free price lists and flyers.
Gooleni 11 Riverside Dr. Suite 5 VE New York, N.Y. 10023	Seashells of many varieties.	
Greentree Ranch Wools Countryside Handweavers 163 N. Carter Lake Rd. Loveland, Colo. 80537	Wide variety of fat yarns as well as traditional yarns.	Price list free.
Grey Owl Indian Craft Mfg. Co., Inc. 150–02 Beaver Rd. Jamaica, Queens, N.Y. 11433	American Indian craft supplies.	Catalog: $.25.
P. C. Herwig Co., Inc. Rt. 2, Box 140 Milaca, Minn. 56353	Linen yarns, sisal, jute, cotton and rayon. Buckles, bells and beads.	Catalog and samples: $.50.

Hollywood Fancy Feather 512 S. Broadway Los Angeles, Cal. 90013	Assorted natural and dyed feathers.	Minimum order: $5.00.
International Handcraft and Supply 32 Hermosa Ave. Hermosa Beach, Cal. 90254	Yarns and cords including goathair, raw silk, leathers. Also assorted beads.	Price list and samples: $1.00, deductible from first order. Minimum order: $5.00. Add tax and shipping costs to all orders.
Lamb's End 165 W. 9 Mile Ferndale, Mich. 48220	Yarns, feathers, beads, seashells.	Yarn samples: $1.00. Minimum order: 1 lb. of fibers.
Las Manos, Inc. 12215 Coitrd (in Olla Podrida) Dallas, Tex. 75230	Imported and domestic yarns, cords, beads and miscellany.	Samples and price list: $.75. Minimum order: $10.00.
Lily Mills Co. Shelby, N.C. 28150	Yarns and threads.	Charge for samples.
Macramé and Weaving Supply Co. 63 E. Adams #403 Chicago, Ill. 60614	Yarns and supplies: beads, belts, seashells, feathers, bones.	Catalog free. Samples: $1.00.
The Mannings–Creative Crafts Handweaving Studio and Supply Center East Berlin, Pa. 17136	Wool, cotton, linen and synthetic yarns; beads, buckles, cords and all miscellaneous macramé supplies. Books.	Catalog and samples: $.50. Minimum order: $5.00.
Naturalcraft 2199 Bancroft Way Berkeley, Cal. 94704	Beads, seashells, feathers, yarns and cordage. Basketry supplies.	Catalog and samples: $.50. Minimum order: $5.00.
Northwest Handcraft House 110 West Esplanade North Vancouver, B.C., Canada	Imported yarns, fleece, raw sisal and manila, dyes, books.	Catalog: $.50.
Oregon Handspun Wool P.O. Box 132 Monroe, Ore. 97456	Handspun yarns.	Samples: $.50.
The Pendleton Shop Handweaving-Knitting Studio 407 Jordan Road P.O. Box 233 Sedona, Ariz. 86336	Yarns, metal rings, buttons, beads.	Send stamped self-addressed envelope for catalog and samples.
Progress Feather Co. 657 W. Lake St. Chicago, Ill. 60606	Assorted feathers. Pelts.	Free price list. Minimum order: $15.00. Wholesale only for quantity purchases.
Rip Neal Threads 9621 Seeley Lake Drive SW Tacoma, Wash. 98499	Assorted threads and yarns. Beads, bells, books.	Price list free.
Tahki Imports, Ltd. 336 West End Ave. New York, N.Y. 10023	Greek, Irish and Colombian handspun yarns.	Free catalog with information for ordering samples.
3 Gables Homecrafts 1825 Charleston Beach Bremerton, Wash. 98310	Handcrafted glazed ceramic beads with large openings.	Free brochure with sample bead. Also wholesale to shops and schools.

Tuxedo Yarn and Needlepoint 36–35 Main St. Flushing, N.Y. 11354	Yarns and supplies. Beads.	Catalog free.
The Unique 21½ East Bijou Colorado Springs, Colo. 80902	Imported yarns and threads.	Sample card: $1.00. Catalog of looms: $1.00. Complete portfolio of yarns, looms and catalogs: $8.00. Price list free.
Warp Woof & Potpourri 514 N. Lake Ave. Pasadena, Cal. 91101	Yarns, beads, buckles, books.	Catalog and samples: $.50.
The Yarn Depot, Inc. 545 Sutter St. San Francisco, Cal. 94102	Assorted yarns, beads, supplies, books, for all crafts.	Samples: $.50 to $1.50. Bimonthly samples club.
The Yarn Loft Upstairs—1442 Camino Del Mar Del Mar, Cal. 92014	Fibers for all crafts. Metallic yarns, canvases, basketry supplies, burlap, suede lacing.	Catalog: $1.00.
Yarn Primitives P.O. Box 1013 Weston, Conn. 06880	Handspun yarns from Greece, Ecuador, Peru, Bolivia, India and Haiti. Wools, goat hair, cotton blends.	Samples: $2.00.

Index

A

Adding Cords, 20, 27, 53, 64–69
Africa, Spike, 198
Akers, Dorris, 5, 69, 81, 185, 199, 201
Al-Hilali, Neda, 10, 67, frontispiece
Alternating Square Knot, 40–41
Anchor Cords, 22
Angled Clove Hitch, 146–49
Animals, 116, 117

B

Baughn, Mary, 59, 149, 182, 195, 199
Beads, 70–77
  Ceramic, 71
  Papier-Mâché, 71
Beaumont, Betty, 183
Belts, 12, 82, 133, 159, 181, 188, 189, 193
Bernard, Eileen, 43, 73, 74, 75
Berry Knot, 150, 151
Bitterman, Sarajane, 82, 131, 133, 189
Black, Virginia, 72, 194
Bottles, 197, 198
Bundles, 18, 52–55
Burchall, Babs, 33, facing 149
Burningham, Charlene, 11, 189
Butterflies, 52–54
Buttons, Square Knot, 51

C

Carlson, Estelle, 53, 94, 96, 97, 99
Carstenjen, Mikael C., 108, 170, 171, 172, 174, 175
Celotex, 14, 18, 187
Ceramics, 7, 173, 174, 175
Chains—Knotting, 134–45
    Clove Hitch, 134–40
    Lark's Head, 141–45
Chinese Crown Knot, 152, 162
Clove Hitch, 3, 4, 11, 22–31, 131–45
    Angled, 146–49
    Chains, 134–40
    Diagonal, 25, 29
    Horizontal, 23, 24
    Leaf Design, 132
    Sliding, 52, 54
    Variations, 130–51
    Vertical, 26–28
Clothing, 13, 149, 169, 180–87, 194, 195
Coil Knots, 78, 79, 152, 163
Coleman, Stana, 76, 77, 169
Color, 18, 19, 53, 61, 62, 63
Cordage Companies, 16
Cords
    Burning, 60
    Estimating Length, 20
    Measuring, 52, 53, 56
    Splicing, 64
Cord Suppliers, 16
Cork, 3, 14, 15, 17, 19
Cotton Twine, 14–19
Crawford, Libby, 91
Creager, Clara, 6, 49, 165
Crouse, Gloria, 100, 103, 115

D

Davidson, Sally, 54, 80, 156, 157, facing 149
Dendel, Esther S., 177, facing 116
Design Ideas, 84–101
Diagonal Clove Hitch, 25, 29
Doran, Lynn, 59, 113
Double Half-Hitch. *See* Clove Hitch
Dumas, Clara S., 6
Dyeing Cords, 53, 61, 62, 63

E

Endings, 78–83
Estimating Cord Lengths, 20

F

Faulkner, John, 113
Ferri, Marion Smith, 68, 88, 101
Fibers
  Man-made, 7, 15
  Natural, 7, 15
Flax, 15
Foster, Mary Sue, 91
Franks, Ron, frontispiece
Fringes, 152, 167, 169
Frinier, Richard, 115
Furnishings, 196–201

G

Gabo, Naum, 97
Geimer, Mary, 109
Glass Blowing, 7, 171, 172
Gluing, 27, 58, 64, 78
Gorski, Berni, 42, 161

H

Half-Knot, 32–51
Half-Knot Twists, 32–50
  Demonstration, 37
Hangings, 2, 5, 6, 10, 22, 30, 31, 33, 42, 43, 46–50, 53, 59, 61, 63, 68, 69, 74,
    81, 83, 84, 86–88, 90–101, 147–49, 161, 165, 168, 176–79
Hardware Stores, 16
Headbands, 131
Hemp, 15, 16
Hennessey, Helen, facing 149
History of Macramé, 4, 7, 8, 157
Hodge, Gerald P., 147
Holding Line, 20, 21
Hoover, Doris, facing 148
Horizontal Clove Hitch, 23, 24
Humphreys, Neva, 86

J

Jewelry, 11, 22, 58, 72, 77, 80, 151, 181, 185
Josephine Knot, 152, 158, 159
Jute, 15–17

K

Kinnell, Judy, 69
Knit Shops, 16
Knot
  Berry, 150, 151

Index

Chinese Crown, 152, 162
Coil, 78, 79, 152, 163
Clove Hitch, 3, 4, 11, 22–31, 131–45
Double Half-Hitch. *See* Clove Hitch
Josephine, 152, 158, 159
Lark's Head, 20, 21, 141–45
Monkey's Fist, 78, 152, 160, 161
Mounting, 20, 21, 188, 190–95
Overhand, 78, 152–55
Square, 3, 4, 11, 32–51
Starting, 20, 21
Knotting Board, 14–19
Knotting Cords, 22
Knotting Strands, 22

L

Lark's Head Knot, 20, 21
Lark's Head Chains, 141–45
Larson, Nancy, 148
Leaf Clove Hitch, 132
Leather, 59
Linen, 15
Littell, Julia, 55, 110, 132, frontispiece
Lobell, Joy, 46, 47, 112, 182

M

Marein, Shirley, 118, 173
Marine Stores, 16
Materials, 14, 15
Measuring Cords, 52, 53, 56
Meilach, Dona, 187, 200, facing 117
Meilach, Susan, 185
Millinery Stores, 16
Monkey's Fist Knot, 78, 152, 160, 161
Montgomery, Rosita, 31, 93, 116
Mounting Knots, 20, 21, 188, 190–95
Muñoz, Aurelia, 2, 30, 95

N

Nylon, 14, 16, 17, 19
Needles, 15
Needham, Lynn, 159, 169, facing 149

O

Ohlson, Lorraine, 171, 178
Origin of Macramé, 3
Ouchi, Michi, 81, 119, 176
Overhand Knot, 78, 152–55

P

Paque, Joan Michaels, 56, 61, 77, 88, 103–5, 133, 144, 145, 148, 151, 152, 194, 196, 197, facing 116, 117
Parada, Esther, 11, 13, frontispiece
Patterns, 187
Pattullo, Antoinette, 63
Pesch, Imelda, 90
Picots, 180, 190–95
Pins, 14–18
Plastic, 16, 58, 59
Platus, Libby, 103, 114, 171, 178, 179
Ply, 17
Polyethelene, 16
Poly-foam, 3
Polypropylene, 16, 17, 19
Polyurethane, 14, 15, 21
Pritchard, Sibyl, 87
Potter, Misty, 195
Purism, 7
Purses, 12, 181, 195

R

Regensteiner, Else, 83, 84
Reverse Lark's Head, 21
Robinson, Esther, 48, 49, 50
Rope, 3, 14–18
Roth, Margaret, 74

S

Sailors, 4, 7, 157
Sampler, 22, 57, 156, 157
Sawyer, Ray W., 188
Schwarcz, LeRoy, 198
Sculpture, 9, 10, 102–29, 170–75
    Demonstration, 106–9
Sekulic, Djordje, 8
Sennits, 32
Seramur, Mary, 117
Sherbeyn, Edward, 181, facing 116
Silk, 15–17
Sisal, 15, 16
Smith, Dorothy, 120
Snidecor, John, 92, 93
Splicing, 64
Square Knot, 3, 4, 11, 32–51
    Buttons, 51
    Demonstration, 34, 35
    Demonstration: alternating pattern, 40–41
Starting Knot, 20, 21

Strecher, Marla, 186
String, 16
Suppliers, Cord, 16

T

Tassels, 78, 152, 166
Textile Arts, 3, 7, 15
Tiffany, Virginia, 168
Todd, Louise, 117, 184, facing 149
Twine, 3, 14–18

V

Vertical Clove Hitch, 26–28

W

Wagner, Peggy, 120, 121, 200
Weaving, 7, 164, 165, 171, 177
Weaving Suppliers, 16
Weaving Warp, 16, 19
Weeks, Corki, 63
Wexler, Joyce, 11, 111
Wire, 58
Working Area, 3, 19
Wrapping, 78, 79

Y

Yarn, 3, 14–18

Z

Zeisler, Claire, 9, 102, 103, 122–29, 183, facing 148
Zelmanoff, Marci, 58, facing 116